European Music Tour with Fast Heart Mart

By "Fast Heart" Martin Stamper

Copyright © 2017 Martin Bryce Stamper. All rights reserved. No part of this publication may be used or reproduced in any manner without written permission from the publisher, except in the case of brief quotations embodied in critical articles and reviews.

Website: fastheartmart.com
Email: fastheartmart@gmail.com

ISBN 10: 1546349146
ISBN 13: 978-1546349143

Interior Formatting: Victor Rook
Cover Design: Roblyn Crawford
Editors: Roblyn Crawford and Beth Pollock

For

Sam Stamper, my cousin. Gone but not forgotten. We quarreled with some of the same monsters. See you on the other side someday.

Beth Pollock, my dear high school creative writing teacher, who gave me the courage to be a writer at a time in my life when I needed it the most.

"Fast Heart" Martin Stamper, San Diego, CA 2016

Chapters

Forward vii
Acknowledgements viii
Introduction ix
Day 1: The European Tour Begins 1
Day 2: Boston To Iceland 3
Day 3: Land Of The Midnight Sun 6
Day 4: Everything Arrived Safely 8
Day 5: What the Heck Am I Going To Eat? 12
Day 6: Reflections 20
Day 7: Zennegat 13 – The Gig At The End Of The Universe! ... 27
Day 8: A Naked German Gig 35
Day 8.5: The Real World - Bremen 41
Day 9: Living The Dream? 45
Day 10: A TV Show, A Concert & A Boatload O' Booty 48
Day 11: Meet The Münsters 53
Day 12: Tillmann Hahn's Gasthaus 57
Day 13: Getting In The Groove At Schwarzer Hermann 62
Day 14: Diaries Are Dangerous 65
Day 15: From A Yurt To A Concert Hall 67
Day 16: Euro Cash 72
Day 17: Here Is The Church, There Is The Steeple. I Showed Up, Now Where's All the People? 75
Day 18: From Point D To Point T 82
Day 19: The Hero Bar 88
Day 20: A Good Review From Berlin 94
Day 21: A Day Off 98
Day 22: Gummy Bears Galore 102
Day 23: Migrant Musician? 103
Day 24: On The Upswing At A Church Concert 107
Day 25: The Most Intimate Concert Yet 111

Day 26: Backstage Divo!... 114
Day 27: Two Encores Tonight!.. 116
Day 28: They Provide the Audience, I Provide the Show........ 117
Day 29: The Grand Finale Concert!... 121
Day 30: Where's Your Cowboy Hat? 124
Day 31: Winding Down.. 129
Day 32: Hello, Köln 131
Days 33 - 37: Sightseein' & Chillin'.. 138
Day 74: Back Home, Safe & Sound... 140
Day 75: Was It All Worth It? 141

Forward

AFTER TRAVELING and playing music together for so many years, Martin and I probably know each other better than we know anyone else. It's an honor to be his friend, to edit his book, and to write this Forward.

Through remarkably candid journaling, Martin shares his struggle with the tensions between creative freedom and monetary success; between physical well-being and industry demands; and between intimate relationships and fleeting fame.

In these pages, we learn a great deal about the Songs & Whispers organization, and the types of perks and pitfalls one may encounter on such a concert circuit. Martin introduces us to an inspired club owner, a jaded journalist, an encouraging apartment painter, an heckling drunk, and dozens of iconic characters, made mysterious by the language barrier, and unfamiliar cultural context.

Guileless, this account is more than a travel log; it's a deeply personal exploration of an emotional landscape. In addition to expressing his unique brand of humor, self-talk, genuine excitement, reigning confusion, and a desire for restraint and routine, Martin courageously unpacks his existential fears, petty jealousies, and revolutionary impulses. Although appearing most vexed by an unrelenting compulsion to question the status quo, which renders him in a constant state of flux, his fans may recognize this fatal flaw as key to the relentless progression of his extraordinary talent.

In the end, this book is valuable not only because we can share what Martin experiences on his trip to Europe, but because Martin's personal reflection helps us to better know, and love, ourselves.

-Roblyn Crawford, January 29, 2017

Acknowledgements

I WOULD LIKE to thank everyone who has ever supported my musical endeavors and me. This includes people who've smiled at me as they walked by me playing in random places. To all the people who've thrown money into my tip jars, and everyone who's bought a CD, or any of my merchandise.

I especially want to thank all the people who supported me, in various ways, on this European tour: Lena Schmidt, Surya, Cherie Stamper, Gene Stamper, Brett Sparks, Stacey Barnett, Kirk Gilliam, Beth Pollock, Andy and Rose Russell, "Whisperin'" Doug Parker, Rebecca Motlagh, Pete Heald, Greg Santogrossi, Patrick Grattan, Rayna Benson, Ronnie Goodman, Andrew Atmatyagi Kutt, Sujantra McKeever, Lance Houghton, Ben Hanna, Peter Dames, Gloria O'Connor, Jamie Sengheiser, Christoph Knerr, Tim Lash, Nikole Fortier, Gregory Page, Julie England, Jane Wheeler, Michael Pelkey, Neil Shambu Vineberg, Steven Vigil, Rachel Habig, Andy Merkel, Mira Ashley, Juniper Bowers, Don Skolnik, Nicole Pisciotto, Jack Johnson (my shrink), and Roblyn Crawford.

Gratitude to Beth Pollock and Roblyn Crawford for all the editing work. I couldn't have finished this book without you.

Introduction

EVERYONE HAS DREAMS. Not everyone attempts to make those dreams a reality. Whether or not we do, is up to each of us.

What follows is a series of journal entries I wrote while making one of my dreams into reality; the dream of playing my music in Europe. I posted these entries to Facebook on the days I wrote them, and people would tell me, "You should make this into a book." So, here I am, organizing the journal entries into a book. Thanks to everyone who told me to do so.

Maybe this book will make some money. Maybe it won't. One day, maybe one of my artistic pursuits will bring in some significant amount of money. Until then, I'll keep on enjoying the ride. I know I'm not getting any younger. As I write this, I'm one month away from turning 40. Some would say I should've given up the dream of being a professional musician long ago. I like to answer them with a quote by a woman named Pam Flowers, "You're never too young to have a dream, and you're never too old to make it come true." Besides, there really isn't much else I want to do with my life.

Excerpt: "It has been said that good music is essentially tension and release. What would that chorus mean without the verse? How interesting could the song be without a minor chord thrown in at just the right moment to help us celebrate the victory over the pain? And so is Life. This is why I've chosen to write these journal entries as honestly as I can. It is our duty as artists to be radically honest now, and face the consequences that may come from that. Consequences make for the tension and release, and within that tension and release exists the consequential beauty."

I sincerely hope you enjoy reading this book!

Day 1: The European Tour Begins

(Because it's just fun to have a huge pink suitcase.)

ALRIGHT! It's been a rollercoaster of emotions this week (welcome back planet Mercury) but I'm full-on excited now! Everything is finally all packed up and ready to go to Germany! It's a significant and chunky tour of concerts I'm booked to perform, and I'm up for the adventure.

I leave tonight at 10:00 p.m. San Diego time. I have a huge pink suitcase, a gigantic backpack with my guitar and banjo in it, and my little briefcase for traveling on the plane. The huge pink suitcase is full of CDs, a battery-powered amp for busking on the streets, my tiny guitar pedal board, very few clothes, miscellaneous music equipment (microphone, cables, etc.), my sleeping bag, and business cards. It's pink so it'll be easy to spot on the airport conveyor belt among the drab black luggage. I'm way more bashful about how much stuff I have packed in the suitcase than the color. I think I usually pack pretty light, but when you're flying across the world to make some money off music, you gotta bring some merchandise to sell and some equipment to conduct business. (Note: The pink suitcase only cost me $8 at a thrift store last week!)

What I'm looking forward to today:
1. Getting through airport security on time and chilling out at the airplane terminal awaiting my airplane to board. Being excited about waiting usually sounds weird, but Life's been so hectic all the time lately that it's gonna be a relief to have nothing to do but wait and talk/text with friends I've been neglecting lately.

Challenges for today:
1. Getting on the airplane on time. The plane ticket says "22:14" (that's 10:14 p.m., right? Why doesn't the USA use the 24-hour clock? It makes so much more sense.)
2. Not getting charged extra for my huge pink suitcase. It's pretty heavy and I'm not sure if the airline is going to charge me extra for it. I'm always amazed airplanes can even get airborne with heavy things like this pink monstrosity on board.
3. Not getting charged extra for my gigantic guitar/banjo case.
4. Getting my guitar and banjo to Germany safely. My backpack is pretty darn good, but I've heard horror stories about instruments getting destroyed. Saying a prayer for the safety of my instruments now!
5. Leaving my van behind. This is my first tour without having a van. My van is my safe haven on tour. I sleep in it. I hide in it. I

sing in it. I cry alone in it. I hope to rent a car in Europe, but I'm still not sure I'll be able to afford it.

I feel blessed to be doing this. It's not easy being a musician these days, but these are the times when it pays off. Thanks to everyone who has donated so far! It's because of you that I can make this trip.

P.S. Even though I haven't left my house yet, I'm gonna consider this Day One of the tour because getting prepared has already been an adventure!

Day 2: Boston To Iceland

(Met up for lunch with my friend Jacob for a layover in Boston)

MEMORIAL DAY, 2016: Thank you to all the people who have served the USA in the name of freedom!

I boarded the plane on time last night in San Diego. I did *not* get charged a fee, thanks to the friendly agent at the check-in who advised me to carry on my CD boxes (as they were making my pink suitcase 13 pounds over-weight.) I'm not sure how my guitar and banjo are doing because I haven't seen them since last night. I'm sending them thoughts of safe passage.

So far, I'm realizing that touring by plane is pretty chill as long as you have plenty of disposable cash to pay $2.50 for a small bottle of water.

I used to tour around the USA in a 1982 vegetable-oil-powered Volkswagen van. It was a magic van, but it was high maintenance and broke down on a regular basis. I would scavenge my own vegetable oil to fuel my tours. There have been few experiences in my entire life that feel as satisfying and liberating as driving on the open road on free fuel that I'd scavenge from the grease dumpsters in the alleys behind restaurants. However, it was a lot of work and stress. By the time I was done preparing vegetable oil or fixing the myriad of mechanical problems that my vegetable-oil-powered van had on a daily basis, I'd have very little vitality and energy left for my music.

In contrast, touring around in airplanes is way more expensive and way less heroic, but in my opinion it's far less stressful. All you gotta do is show up on time and wait. While waiting, I can take care of administrative tasks related to my "music career" (I always use quotes with that phrase because I'm not sure I make enough money to call it a career), and I can catch up with friends and family.

I admit, I do usually require a Xanax when I fly, as I've had some panic attacks on planes in the past (associated with my heart condition.) I think this is because I don't fly very often. If I did, I'd probably get used to being crammed into a tube with 300 other people flying 500 mph at 35,000 feet in the air.

But breaking down in my van in some random place, having to find a rare part from some indeterminate source, and then waiting for its delivery (with no guarantee that it will fix the problem) while trying to get to a show on time is also stressful.

I wouldn't trade the days of vegetable-oil-van-touring for anything. They were adventurous as can be. I remember during one tour, my starter was out the entire time, and I had to push-start the van for four entire weeks. In the middle of Wyoming, one of my vegetable oil filters clogged while I was driving through a one-lane construction zone on a freeway that had barricades on both sides and no shoulder to pull over. My Diesel engine stalled out, and the only way I could start it again was to switch from the vegetable oil tank over to the diesel tank and pop the clutch at 50 mph! It took about five attempts at popping the clutch, and I was down to about 20 mph with a line of traffic behind me (at least 20 cars and big rigs deep) when the little Diesel engine finally started up again! Now *that* was stressful, but what a story!

Perhaps someday I'll return to that low-budget, environmentally responsible way of touring, but for now, I'm glad I've graduated to airplane touring, so I can focus more on my music.

I think those days of vegetable-oil-van touring have taught me to handle airplane touring rather well. I have a return ticket back to the USA for the end of July. Everything else seems manageable. I just need to make enough money with my music to pay my bills back home and to survive this tour. Life is under control. Iceland here I come!

What I'm looking forward to today:
Seeing my friend Jacob who's a native Bostonian. I have such a long layover that he's gonna meet me at the airport for lunch!

Challenges for today:
1. Getting enough sleep and rest without a bed. Kind of exhausted already from having to sleep hunched over my tray

table last night, in between two antisocial people, and in front of someone who snored like they were hacking up loogies all night. Today, I paid $25 for a neck pillow, so hopefully that helps me sleep on the way to Iceland tonight.

2. Switching to an international terminal in Boston, and catching my plane to Iceland on time.

Day 3: Land Of The Midnight Sun

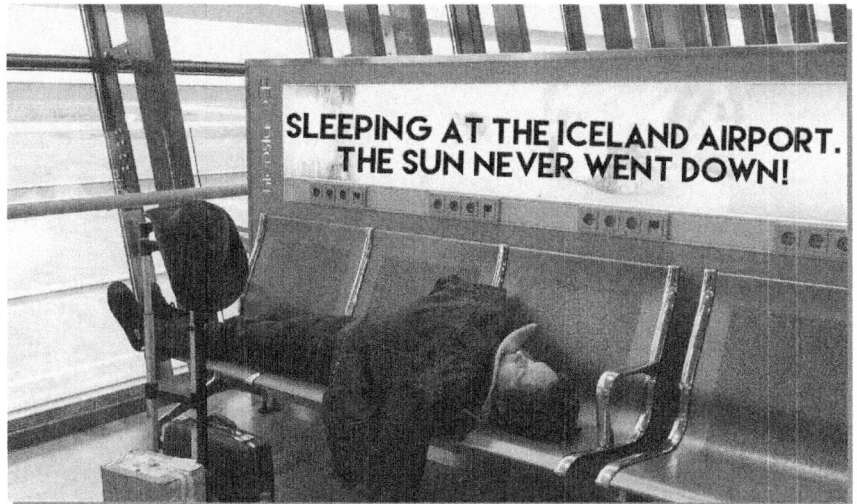

(Cue "Immigrant Song" by Led Zeppelin)

LAST NIGHT I witnessed the Land of the Midnight Sun as I transferred planes at Reykjavík, Iceland airport. It was really pretty surreal and discombobulating to see an orange sunset at midnight, illuminating the exotic Icelandic landscape.

Icelandic Airlines has quite a sense of humor! I can't think of any specific examples at the moment, except that their flight safety instructional video was conducted with a woman in a beautiful landscape far away from any planes. Also, their food menu had some subtle humor that made me laugh. I hope this sense of humor continues throughout Europe as I think it'll mean people will get me much better.

I had an eight-hour layover in Reykjavík. I tried to lie down and sleep in an attempt to acclimate to the time changes (and get a jump on resolving any jet lag I may have.) However, maybe the metal bench wasn't comfortable enough? Or the sun shining at 1:00 a.m. threw off my sleep activation? I was not able to get any proper sleep.

Anyway, I just now arrived in Hamburg, Germany! I've been napping for short bursts on airport benches, and airplanes (sometimes with my head down on my tray table like a rebellious teenager in a high school classroom), for about 48 hours. I'm feeling pretty haggard and out of it at the moment, but I'm grateful to be here.

What I'm looking forward to today:
1. Lying down in a bed and not being in an airplane or at an airport (with the pressure of catching another airplane flight.)
2. Checking in with the "Songs and Whispers" agency in Bremen that booked and promoted this tour

Challenges for today:
1. Get rid of jet lag ASAP
2. Rest up enough to feel inspired to play music
3. Decide whether to take a train, bus, or to rent a car
4. Navigate my way from Hamburg to Bremen
5. Make sure my guitar and banjo made it safely

Day 4: Everything Arrived Safely

INCLUDING ME! I mustered the nerve to look inside my instrument case. My guitar and banjo have arrived in Germany unharmed! That's incredible considering I can hardly schlep this guitar/banjo backpack case from the airport to the car without feeling like I'm going to smash into a wall, or just get frustrated at having such a huge backpack.

The plane ride from Iceland to Hamburg, Germany went ok. I stumbled onto the plane sleep deprived. I put my cardboard boxes and cart in the overhead compartment as gracefully as I could, but I imagined I still looked pretty clumsy to all the people waiting behind me with their neat little roll-on luggage. These are the boxes that I had to get out of my pink suitcase because they were making it too heavy and they were going to charge me $140 extra. The ladies next to me on the plane weren't very friendly. I'm not sure if it's because of how I boarded the plane and took so much time to get my stuff in the overhead or what? I made what I thought was a funny joke when I sat down.

"Wow, these seats have lots of leg room."

"That's because we are in the emergency exit row," the lady

answered, with a look of "are you worthy of this position?"

"Fine with me," I answered, with my best look of heroic confidence. Then the Xanax kicked in and I fell asleep for the next three hours, only to be awakened by the stewardess asking of I'd like something to eat, which I did not.

I arrived at the Hamburg Airport in a foggy state of mind. I retrieved my luggage from the conveyor belt and headed for the exit. (Did you know "exit" in German is "ausfahrt"? That's logical to me. Ass-fart = Exit. Ha!) When I came out to the arrivals section, there were so many people huddled around the gate, awaiting their loved ones. I have not seen this very much in the USA in a long time. Perhaps the German people still value family and friends, and make the time for them (unlike in the USA, where we've all lost the time for such things?)

I sat in the terminal with all my gear, trying to decide how to get to Bremen, a city about 90 miles away from Hamburg. Bremen is the city I will be playing in the most on this tour. It's the location of both the Songs And Whispers booking agency and the artist flat where I'll be staying. I decided to rent a car, as the owner of Songs and Whispers informed me that it would be nearly impossible to do the tour on public transportation.

I was reluctant to rent a car. First, it's not cheap, and I feel like I've spent a fortune on this tour already. Also, I've always heard the public transportation in Europe is so great that I wanted to take advantage of it. Alas, I am from the USA, and have to admit that I love having the freedom of a car.

I went online to see what I could find. It was inconclusive, so instead, I gathered my luggage, and headed over to the rental car area of the airport. There are about eight rental car places to choose from. I visited six of them before narrowing down my search for the best deal. I walked back and forth between the final three choices about four times because more questions kept coming up. Some of the sales people at the counters did not have a sense of humor about this, so I ruled them out as possibilities.

After about two hours of the negotiations and going off to think it through, I finally rented a car for €1016 for the month. That's about $1130! (Half as much as all the rest of the places after all the taxes and insurance, but still, I'm really starting to question what's going on here?) This is all a lot of money for me and only made possible because my kind friends and fans donated their own money.

Am I on vacation or a business trip? The answer is neither and both. I have all the responsibilities of a business trip, but no guaranteed pay; with all the expenses of a vacation, but no guaranteed relaxation. Whatever. I'm a musician. Who knows?

I loaded up the tiny car. I have been able to sleep in every car I've taken on tour in the past, but this little Toyota Yaris will be the exception. I can just barely fit all my gear in there with me. Even if I didn't have all the gear, the way the back seats fold down would not allow me to lie down.

I looked up the address of where I was going to meet my liaison from Songs and Whispers, and drove out to Bremen. I have a very limited data plan on my phone, so I'm reluctant to use the GPS. But I have to have something to help me navigate.

I drove on the Autobahn for the first time today! Holy Mackrel! I've never seen cars coming into my rear view mirror so fast… and consistently. On other highways, you get some maniac going 150 mph once or twice a year. On the Autobahn, it's going on all the time. I'm into it though! If I had a fast car, I'd want to drive it fast. However, my little Toyota rental tops out at about 110 kph, which, now that I do the calculations, is only approximately 70 mph. Hmmmm. Not sure what's up with that?

I met up with my liaison, Arne, from Songs and Whispers. What a great and kind guy. As I arrived after hours, he invited me into his apartment. He wanted to make sure I got into my artist flat, so I could get some sleep. Arne and I talked for about an hour (about the tour I'll be doing, German topics, etc.) before I headed over to the artist flat.

I arrived just in time to meet Pi Jacobs. Pi Jacobs is an artist from the previous tour, and she had done her last performance tonight in Hamburg. Pi is out of Los Angles, and she caught me up on things. We exchanged stories before calling it a night. I probably came off to her sounding way too negative and jaded about being a musician. Why do I let myself come across like this? What do I want? Where am I going? I gotta figure out my life already. Or maybe I'm just tired. The adventure continues.

What I'm looking forward to today:
1. Getting organized and settled in for the tour
2. Having two days of downtime to do very little

Challenges for today:
Jet lag. I'm feeling good so far, so hopefully I'm gonna be ready for my first performance on Friday in Belgium.

Day 5: What the Heck Am I Going To Eat?

I AWOKE to the peaceful sound of birds and children playing this morning. The birds were cooing and chirping in the canopy of green trees beside my third story window, and the children were yelling at each other in German. The landscape outside my window, on this June 1st day, reminds me of my childhood in Virginia during the summer. I currently reside in the Southern California desert of San Diego, where trees are rare, so it was pleasant to wake up with this green scene outside my window. It rained last night, with a little bit of lightning, and there was a misty fog surrounding the scenery. The houses in the neighborhood where I'm staying look like the government housing in the States. They're huge four-story brick buildings, probably built in the early 1900's, with nice community areas of grass, trees, and children's playgrounds, between them. Apparently, this is a section of town heavily populated with immigrants from all over the world, especially Syrian refugees. There's even a bike trail that fellow artist Pi Jacobs pointed out to me before she left for The Netherlands.

I woke up at 4:00 a.m. (locally) this morning. The sun was already up. I only slept about four hours last night, but I decided to get up and to be as productive as possible. I know from experience, the best way for me to deal with insomnia is to go about my day as if I had slept all night. Hopefully, I'll work up an exhausted sleep for tonight. I caught up on email correspondence, unpacking, and getting situated in the artist flat. The artist flat is now empty, except for me. The rest of the musicians for this tour are still not here yet. Some are coming from San Francisco, and the others are coming from Australia. We will share some concerts together, but for the most part, it seems we'll be on our own (only meeting at the flat between shows, etc.) The Songs and Whispers artist flat is where all the artists on the tour stay. There are three bedrooms, six beds, a kitchen, and a skinny bathroom with an enormous bathtub, deep enough for a toddler to swim. I don't have a bathtub at my apartment in San Diego, so I plan on utilizing this one while I'm here. Although the weather is so warm I may not desire a hot bath, except in the very early mornings when the rest of the artists will probably be asleep.

I am a morning person. I love getting up early in the morning, especially when I've had adequate sleep. I find the morning is my best time to create. Being a morning person can be counterproductive to the typical musician's lifestyle. It may be strange, but I really prefer afternoon and early evening concerts, because I like to be in bed by 11:00 p.m. As soon as the sun starts to wane, so do I. It can be frustrating at times, if I have a late night performance and get to bed late, because I seem to wake up with the sun. Even if I go to sleep at 2:00 a.m., I typically still wake up at 6:00 a.m. Still, I think it's a pretty healthy way to be.

I helped Pi out to her car and said goodbye. She's done with the tour now. She's off to play a festival in The Netherlands. Before she left, she informed me that she's signed to a record label in Floyd, Virginia! Floyd, Virginia seems like a good place, and I'm sad I've never been there, especially since I'm from Virginia. I'll put it on the list of places to go.

As Pi was leaving, a cleaning crew of two ladies came in and then left within about an hour. Then a painter arrived to paint the bathroom. I let him into the apartment. I tried to communicate with him, but when he found out I only speak English, he kind of ignored me and went straight to working. I had finished showering by the time he arrived, which was perfect, because he made a huge mess of the bathroom (chips of paint and wall now filling the bathtub.)

I had unstrung my instruments for the flight, thinking it would keep them safer. I even took the tuners off my banjo. I was stringing them up again and playing a little bit, when the painter came to my bedroom door, smiling. He looked at me gleefully, and spoke, obviously praising my music in German, and making guitar-strumming motions.

"Do you speak English?" I asked. He shook his head, no. I pulled out the German phrase book that my friend had given me. The painter and I looked up words and phrases to communicate with each other.

"*Ich bin* Fast Heart Mart," I told him. He thought this was great, as he smiled really big and answered that his name is Ricardo. This scene went on for about 40 minutes. He loved my music and seemed to admire my abilities. Ricardo eventually left, saying he would return at 7:30 a.m. tomorrow morning. This interaction with Ricardo made me realize that he could have been the nicest, kindest man in the world, but the language barrier stopped me from realizing it either way. Ricardo was talking enthusiastically to me, but I had no idea what he was saying.

I met up again with Arne (my liaison from the agency), this

time at the Songs and Whispers headquarters, which looks exactly like I had imagined. It has a stereotypical "headquarters" look, with lots of glass walls separating the various desks there. I joked that it looked like an episode of the TV show "Mad Men" or an old detective show from the 50's. I met the owner of the Songs and Whispers agency, Heiko, while I was there. All the employees of the company were very friendly and happy to see me. They seem to work constantly on booking and promoting all the artists that come through. I've never seen anything like it in all my days of being a DIY (Do it Yourself) musician.

I drove back to the artist flat after my meeting with Arne. I was pretty groggy with jet lag and lack of sleep, but I get the feeling that driving around Bremen and Germany is not always easy. There's all these narrow two-way streets that are really only wide enough to be one-way streets, and sometimes the sidewalks come jutting out into your lane with a triangular sign (that may be a yield sign), and I think you're supposed to yield to oncoming traffic until the way is clear? Traffic circles are fun, but they are everywhere, and sometimes I don't even realize I'm in one! There are lots of bicyclists and pedestrians. My iPhone GPS reads me the directions, but the street names are so long and foreign to me that it's tricky figuring it all out.

Arriving back at the flat, I realized I hadn't really eaten much up until that point, and I was getting hungry. I decided to walk to the grocery store that Pi recommended.

I'm a picky eater. I really prefer to eat vegan when possible. I don't like avocados all that much, although I tolerate them. I really like eggs. I hear they're the most efficient form of protein on the planet. I think dairy is gross. It's mammary juice from a cow. How is that not gross? Especially if it's rotted into cheese! If a new cure came about to save the whales by milking them, would we drink and eat that whale milk? Unless you live as a hunter-gatherer, meat is archaically cruel, and hard on the environment with the overpopulated world we live in today. I'll eat chicken, if there are no other options, and some beef, when push comes to shove, but I never eat pork. I think Samuel Jackson in "Pulp Fiction" said it best, "I don't dig on swine."

Inside the grocery store, I quickly realized that almost none of the labels are in English. In the produce section, I could not tell what was organic and what was not. I picked out some cherries and pears, and moved on to the rest of the store. What was I looking for? Q: What do I usually eat back home? A: Fruit for breakfast, soup or a sandwich for lunch. I go out to dinner with friends a lot, but if I stay home, I'll eat rice and beans with vegetables. I think I walked around the store about five times trying to figure out what to buy. I must have looked like someone on psychedelics or something, if anyone was watching. I had a lost look of curiosity and annoyance on my face. I felt like I was hallucinating a little bit because I was so hungry and the fluorescent lighting in there was getting to me after 35 minutes of walking in circles around all the aisles in the store. I looked everywhere for rice. I found lots of noodles, but no rice (I avoid gluten when possible.) I did not see any beans. I did find cans of what I surmised to be vegetarian chili. The sight of this vegetarian chili was a relief! I put four cans in my basket. I really don't even know if it was vegetarian chili as I couldn't read the label, but I deduced that the word *"Vegetarisch"* on the label must mean "vegetarian," and that *"Chili sin Carne"* must mean "without meat," just like it does in Spanish. I decided to forget looking for rice and instead looked for corn chips. None! Nada! Zilch! There were some small bags of corn chips with flavoring on them, but I couldn't read the labels on them to find out if the flavoring has MSG in it, or other things that I avoid. I started to panic a little bit, dizzy, and spinning around all the aisles. The hallucinogenic feeling intensified the longer I stayed under the fluorescent lights. As I became hungrier, I started to have visions of a news story: "Fast Heart Mart Goes to Germany: Starves to death before even playing one single show."

I thought I'd abort the grocery store mission and go find a Chinese restaurant. Chinese food is my favorite, because it's usually pretty easy to find a Chinese restaurant that will simply serve me rice and vegetables. On my phone, I yelped the term "Chinese food." The closest was two miles away. I yelped any restaurant, and the closest seemed to be a mile away. I wasn't sure I'd be able to find anything to eat there, and I did not have the energy to walk, nor the patience to drive. I don't eat fast food a lot, but if there were a fast food place nearby, I would have gone there. There was not even a McDonald's, which is pretty impressive, actually. I had no choice but to continue my mission at the grocery store.

In the grocery store, there were rows and rows of candy and alcohol, yet nary a grain of rice, nor a chip of corn. I had found some parsley and arugula to add to my vegetarian chili. I found some €0.20 sparkling water, a Snickers bar, and some salt and vinegar potato chips.

After a long time, and too many circles of the grocery store (passing a mother and her baby who seemed to be just as lost as me, but looked at me as if I had no excuse to be), I decided to head to the cashier. The cashier held up my carton of eggs with a quizzical look, as if she were looking for the price tag. I deduced that she had asked me, "How much are these eggs?" in German. "I don't know," I answered in English. She sent a girl to do a price check. The line behind me grew as we waited. I noticed there were no bags at the cashier stand, so I pulled out my iPhone and looked up the German word for "bag," as we waited for the price check girl to return.

"Tasche?" I asked, motioning an invisible atmosphere around my groceries. She said something in German and pointed behind me to the bags for sale. A brown paper bag was €0.99 (approximately $1.00.) I bought a cloth bag for €2.00. Wow! No plastic bags here! That's impressive. I mean, I like having plastic bags around for all sorts of reasons like free trash bags, but I can

respect not having them around, nor giving them away for free. After all, there apparently is an island somewhere in the ocean now that's made of all the plastic that got away (I call it "Polymer Island.")

As I walked back to the artist flat, on the bike path that meanders through the trees, I wondered how the heck I find myself in these crazy situations in Life? Is this going to be like when I toured New Zealand in 2007, and all I ate were French fries and beer? All I wanted to do was play some music. It's not that complicated. Now I'm starving and I can't communicate in a language that I've never had a desire to speak. I've never desired to speak any foreign languages. In fact, I've always been particularly bad at foreign languages. I failed every foreign language class I ever took in high school. I can hardly speak English sometimes. I just want to play some songs and get on with Life. I can't wait to get back to the flat and chill out with my food and some Netflix. That's when I happened upon a somewhat miraculous and precious scene.

A man was sitting at a park bench, unabashedly drinking a beer. He looked like he was homeless, as he was pretty dirty and haggard. I haven't seen many homeless people in Germany so far. About 20 feet away from him sat a policeman meditating on another park bench. Somehow this represented the yin-yang of Life to me (total opposites that somehow need each other.) The two men were certainly aware of each other; tolerating each other; validating each other's existence. For some reason I found it special.

Back at the artist flat, I entered the door and was greeted by someone that I assumed was another artist. "Hi, I'm Fast Heart Mart," I shook the man's hand. He spoke to me in German and started to turn away from me, as if in fear that he had no idea what was going on. He said his name was Chris though. I walked into the kitchen and there was a girl cleaning the windows. She spoke a little English and told me her name. I deduced that they were the crew cleaning the flat. I went to my room with my groceries because I wanted to stay out of their way. Then the girl came to my room and started cleaning my windows. I felt in the way, so I went to hang out in another room. The man then came into that room with a vacuum cleaner and I went to a third room. Then the man came into *that* room, so I went to the kitchen and smashed myself into a corner next to their cleaning supplies until they were done. I could have gone outside to my car, but it was pretty hot out, and I was starving. I just wanted to eat. I wanted to speak to the cleaning crew, but I didn't know how, and I was not in the mood to pull out my German phrase book. They left about 30 minutes after I arrived. I ate some vegetarian chili, texted with friends back home, and corresponded on social media.

Tonight was kind of a lonely night, but I know this is a passing phase and I'm cherishing this downtime. I have a feeling that, once this tour starts, I'll be pretty busy all the time. I also have a feeling I'll be eating a lot of canned vegetarian chili while I'm here in Germany. The sun went down at about 10:00 p.m. *Guten Nacht.*

What I'm looking forward to tomorrow:
1. Getting acclimated to the time difference
2. Getting excited to be on tour with my music

Challenges for tomorrow:
1. Sleeping
2. Eating healthy

Day 6: Reflections

(German graffiti in English!)

SINCE I CAN REMEMBER, songs have been really important to me. I remember singing country songs in my parents' car in the early 80's when we were driving around. "The Gambler," and "Lucille," by Kenny Rogers; "Elvira," by the Oak Ridge Boys; and "Flowers on the Wall," by the Statler Brothers are a few that I recall right now, but I know there were many more that I enjoyed.

When I was about eleven, sometimes I would pass out for no reason. Also, there were a rash of sudden deaths on my dad's side of the family. My cousin died at the age of 12, and my aunt was 31 when she died one morning, unexpectedly. I would wonder, sometimes, if I was next. I think that kind of made me an anxious kid. Some doctors wondered if it was just my anxiety making me pass out. My parents took me to neurologists, cardiologists, psychologists; you name it. None of them could explain why. I did not like going to the psychologists, as it made me feel like a weirdo! I got pretty sad, and would sit in my room and listen to music by myself. That's when the idea hit me: I wanted to be a rock star! I figured that rock stars get to work out their anxieties in front of the world, and that's what I wanted to do. I'd always loved singing and the peace and calm it brought me. I sold all my radio-controlled cars, and bought an electric guitar. I would write songs, and sing them in my room, alone. I did not tell anybody that I wanted to be a rock star someday, as I thought they would laugh. Maybe I didn't really even admit it to myself.

When I was seventeen, I passed out again in the hallway at school. When I came to, there was blood everywhere from my front teeth being knocked out because I hit the ground face first. Everyone thought I was dead, and they were kind of freaking out. I've been told that I was legally dead. I did not "see the light," but I was very disappointed to come back to this reality. I felt like, "Oh no, *this* place again?" Whatever is on the other side felt much more peaceful. This was when a doctor finally diagnosed my passing out problem as a heart condition called *Long QT Syndrome*. It's basically an electrical problem that makes my heart quiver instead of pumping blood. So it's not technically a "fast heart," but it kind of is. The doctors installed a defibrillator to shock my heart back into rhythm when I needed it.

I was planning on going into the military after high school. I did not like school very much, and I knew I didn't want to go to college. I was very active, jogging ten miles everyday, riding my bike everywhere, lifting weights, etc. I wanted to be a Navy Seal, if possible. However, the military would not accept me with a heart condition.

I became very confused at this time. Why is the world so inhospitable? Why do people have to work so much and seem so miserable? Why does everyone drive a car everywhere when they know it's destroying the planet? Why are there so many of us people? Where can a person go who wants to live free and off the land?

I had a friend from high school who was also very confused from a traumatic thing that had happened in his life. We decided to strap on some backpacks and hike the Appalachian Trail. While out on the trail, I was approached by some gruff thru-hiker.

"What's your trail name?" I didn't respond because I didn't have one. "You gotta have a trail name, or else we're gonna think you're narcs."

"Fast Heart Mart," I quickly replied, not wanting to be outcaste. I gave a name that had been bouncing in my head since I was diagnosed with the erratic heart condition.

My friend and I did not stay on the Appalachian Trail forever like we had planned, so I reluctantly went to community college (if only to be eligible for my parents' health insurance coverage.) After all, the defibrillator implanted in my chest cost about $40,000, so I figured I better be covered.

I had developed a loathing of sitting in classrooms, as I feared that I would pass out in front of everyone and cause a scene, like I had done so many times before. Also, I saw the education system as somewhat of a farce, because it wasn't necessarily about obtaining knowledge, just remembering some facts to regurgitate for a test and then forget; a place to jump through hoops for professors so you can get a job; to pay a lot of money, and then repay all that money with interest that goes to the wealthy.

"You wanna live a good life?" I imagined the fat cat with the cigar and a top hat asking. "Here's some money. Go to school and learn some things that I approve of you knowing, and then pay me back with interest. Then, you'll have a good job, and have a good life."

In 1999, I moved to Albuquerque, New Mexico, and attended the University of New Mexico. I was a broke student, and was tired of eating bean burritos. I wanted to take my girlfriend out to eat a great meal.

"Why don't you go play some of your songs on the college campus for all the people walking by?" my friend suggested. "They will like your songs and throw tip money at you."

"I'm not a beggar," I replied.

"It's not begging," he retorted, "it's playing music and making the world a more beautiful place."

Remember, this was 1999. Back then, in Small Town USA, there weren't that many people playing music out on the streets like there are now.

I gave it a shot. I went to the UNM campus, put out my guitar case, and started singing. Sure enough, I made enough to take my girlfriend out to dinner! Furthermore, a man who owned a local cafe heard me, and booked me to play my first show ever!

That's all it took to make sense to me: I wanted to be a rock star (or at least a singer/songwriter who made enough money to live.) I did not believe in the higher education system (I was panicked to sit in a classroom), and I had people who wanted to hear me play music. Sure, I could have stayed in college, finished my Bachelor's degree (B.S. ha ha!), and had something to "fall back on." But as a life-long professional musician told me, "If you have something to fall back on, then you *will.*" A few months later, I dropped out of college to pursue my music, and "I never looked back." Just kidding. I've looked back so many times, I think I've had a hard time moving forward. The music business is tricky. It's not like you can just go pay college tuition, fake your way to a degree, and get a job making money. In the music business (and the arts in general), you have to win the hearts of people if you're ever going to get anywhere. Sure, there are the contrived exceptions of the mega pop stars out there. I'm not gonna mention any names, as I don't think that's necessary, but mostly you have to prove yourself and your skills. To say, "I've never looked back," would be a lie. It's a scary path to walk, and I often wonder if I should turn around. Can I turn around?

That was over 15 years ago now. I have played lots of street corners, open mics, cafes, house concerts, bars, a few huge concert halls, festivals, etc. I have opened for some great acts: The Handsome Family, Beck (twice, outside the venues on the street… but he did thank me once for "opening" for him), Calexico, Railroad Earth, and many of my friends' bands. I have recorded over 10 albums! I realize now, that I need to pull it together. I love being a musician! I need a great song, a great recording, and a "big break!" I feel like the music has invited me to follow this path, and I happily abide.

Every time I think, "That's it. My music career is gone. I'm going to pack it up," I get a call from a producer saying they want to use my music in a film, or a great show opportunity comes along, or a fan writes me a message saying how much my music means to them, or just something lures me back. This time, it has been the Songs And Whispers tour circuit here in Bremen, Germany.

I did not even realize that I had been picked for a tour with Songs and Whispers, until a musician from Boulder, Colorado named Ben Hannah, contacted and congratulated me! I didn't know Ben Hanna at the time when he originally wrote me, in August of 2015, so I checked out his website. I instantly fell in love with his song and video "High Society Scene." Ben and I have been friends since then, and check in with each other periodically.

Initially, I wondered if the Songs and Whispers circuit was a hoax, because there are so many scams out there to get money out of musicians. It's weird, because not a lot of unknown musicians have money, but there are vampires out there trying to feed off musicians nonetheless. Songs and Whispers had found me on "ReverbNation" (another company whose legitimacy I questioned.) As I looked more into Songs and Whispers, I found them to be a legitimate company. Ben Hanna found them legit, because he knew the owner, Heiko, through a songwriter scene in Boulder, Colorado. Songs and Whispers even has a Wikipedia page. I really like Wikipedia, and I've come to trust them. I even donate to them every year.

I had never been to Europe before. I'd always heard good things about it, especially for buskers, so I decided to do my best to gather the funds to make a Songs and Whispers tour happen.

While I started to prepare for the tour, I was simultaneously accepted for a home loan in the Joshua Tree area of California. It's been a dream of mine, for a long time, to own a home in the desert, and travel for the summer playing my music. I thought it was finally manifesting. However, I still had a great full time job working as a videographer/audio producer for a great company called "Pilgrimage of the Heart Yoga" in San Diego, and playing in their *Kirtan* band (Kirtan music is a form of music that is usually simple chants of spiritual inspiration. It's been a blessing to be in the band.) Therefore, the last 10 months of my life have been pretty hectic: preparing for a German tour; buying a house in Joshua Tree; working my job for Pilgrimage of the Heart; performing and writing my music; and trying to have a social life of some kind.

I've always had a day job. I don't mind day jobs. I think I just would like to have more time off (maybe three months a year?) I think the reason I haven't gone further with my "music career" is because I've always had to work a day job. Leonard Cohen, Bob Dylan, Neil Young all come from wealthy families, and I don't think they ever worked day jobs. Maybe being a musician is for children of the aristocracy? I'm kind of kidding here, but dang! The day jobs are distracting. You know what else is distracting? Broken hearts! I've had so many broken hearts it's been hard to focus on getting ahead with my music. Anyway, that's that.

Fast forward to now: June 2, 2016. I quit my job at Pilgrimage of the Heart Yoga to come to Germany. I had to leave the Pilgrimage of the Heart Kirtan band, indefinitely. The house in Joshua Tree is still in escrow. It's been an eight-month-long exercise in existential despair, because the bank has been particularly disrespectful in keeping the short sale moving. I'm in Germany, and I still don't know if the deal will ever go through, even though I've signed all the final papers and loan documents.

For a long time now, I've been asking the Universe to send me a booking and promotion agent. I love writing songs. I love playing music. I don't love a whole lot else about the music business, especially booking and self-promotion. I did not imagine that my request to the Universe would be answered by a company all the way in Bremen, Germany, but isn't that always the way? The answer comes in the least expected ways.

So, here I am: going back to music full-time. I've heard that Europeans love music (especially *avant-garde* music.) Maybe I'll even return to the USA with a lot more artistic credibility? Even Jimi Hendrix had to come to England before people took him seriously in the USA. All I have to concentrate on now is playing my music, and that's fine with me. Overall, after the money is spent/invested/squandered on this trip, I hope to be re-inspired to be a musician!

What I'm looking forward to tomorrow:
1. My first show of the tour
2. My first show in Europe
3. My only show in Belgium on this tour

Challenges for tomorrow:
1. Finding the venue. The venue is notoriously difficult to find, according to artists from previous tours. And it's a five-hour drive from Bremen (260 miles is a lot for Europe.) Wish me well!
2. Driving on the Autobahn again. I'm gonna stay all the way to the right as much as possible (to keep my slow car from getting rear-ended by all the Audis and Mercedes driving 150 mph.)

Day 7: Zennegat 13 – The Gig At The End Of The Universe!

THE JET LAG is subsiding, but I didn't sleep very well last night. I woke up a lot, tossed and turned, and then finally got to sleep (but woke up later than I'd like, feeling tired and a bit discombobulated). I trudged on with my day anyway, as any great traveling musician does.

My first flat mates have arrived: Georgina Ward, and her crew (her boyfriend, Danny, and her guitar player, Ripley.) They are Australian and I love them already. It's only been a few days of being in a country where English isn't the dominant language and I'm feeling isolated in some ways – as though I can't truly connect with the people around me. Georgina and her crew are the perfect cure for that!

My mom is from Christchurch, New Zealand. I've been to New Zealand twice and I have a half-sister there, and relatives.

Georgina reminds me of my sister in New Zealand a lot, which is nice because my sister in New Zealand is a lot of fun. My sister's name is Gina. Coincidence?

Georgina Ward and her Australian crew really livened up the flat! I'm looking forward to hanging out with them more. However, today I had to leave at about 11:00 a.m. for my first European gig at *"Zennegat 13"* in Belgium, 261 miles away.

As I said before, Zennegat 13 is a notoriously difficult gig to find. At the artist flat, there's a log with reviews of all the gigs on the circuit, written by the previous musicians. Some gigs get good ratings. Some gigs get bad ratings. Some gigs get mixed reviews. Zennegat 13 is almost unanimously reviewed as something like, "Difficult to find, but once I was there it was a great show." I even read one review that said, "I gave up looking for the place." One review of the Zennegat 13 was, "The gig at the end of the Universe."

As I left the flat there was a photographer taking photos of the flat for some publication. She looked like she may be a famous photographer, because she was eccentric with her straw cowboy hat (I haven't seen many cowboy hats in Germany) and her beige Crocs (shoes.) Also, she had an agent/manager escorting her around. I wish I would have jumped into the photo that she was taking of my humongous guitar case, but all I was thinking about at the time was getting on the road, because I had a feeling it was going to be a long journey finding Zennegat 13. Dang! Hindsight is 20/20. I could've had the best publicity photo ever. Take that as a lesson form your Uncle Fast Heart Mart kids, always be present and seize every opportunity (as opposed to being completely consumed by Zennegat 13.)

I packed my gigantic pile of musical equipment into my tiny car before heading out: huge guitar/banjo case; small briefcase/merchandise case; small amp (supplied by Songs and Whispers); big box of stage lights and cords (provided by Songs and Whispers); one grocery bag of food; one grocery bag of clothes/toiletries; laptop computer; and a sleeping bag. It's hard to see out my back window once all this is in the tiny car, but maybe that's better, as I won't get as stressed out by all the tailgaters?

I'm using my iPhone's GPS to navigate around Germany. So far, I'm reluctant to use it, because I know it's going to suck down my data on my AT&T "International Passport" cell phone plan, but what the heck else can I do? Use an analog map? Yikes! I'm not sure I'd know how anymore. Besides, I'm a bit afraid to admit it, but it's kind of comforting to have Siri's voice with me in my solo car trips in a foreign land like this. Perhaps if I had someone with me, we could use analog maps, but I'm gonna stick to using my iPhone.

The drive to Zennegat 13 was exhausting! Turns out, Friday traffic in Europe is almost as bad as it is in the USA. Plus, all the Autobahn drivers stress me out pretty quick with their tailgating and demanding speeds. Good news though, I got the Toyota Yaris/Aygo up to about 150 kph! I must have had a bad head wind the other night when I didn't seem to be able to go over 110 kph. Whoa! I just did the calculation: 150 kph = about 90 mph! Dang, that's probably too fast to be going in this tiny car. I'll try and stay around 110 kph.

I took a few wrong turns at times, and Siri had to reroute me on some detours. Stopping for fuel was weird, because I wasn't sure how to read the signs to know where to exit. Then I had a hard time knowing how to legally get in and out of the gas station, as there are these automatic gates that go across the road. Plus, there are one-way streets, and I didn't know which side of my car to pump the fuel. I had to meander through a bunch of pumps for big rig trucks to find the pump for small/regular/passenger cars. When I finally went in to prepay, the kid there was friendly and spoke in English. He laughed, "Oh no, you fuel first, then come in and pay." I wanted to buy a sub sandwich from the kid, but I couldn't read the signs well enough.

I went across the parking lot to Burger King, because I figured I'd know what I was ordering.

Burger King is a giant corporation that I do not want to support, but damn, I was tired of swimming upstream. I went in and ordered a #4 Chicken Sandwich and fries, and a bottle of sparkling water (because the cashier insisted that I should get a drink.) I don't drink soda (sugar) and she thought I was silly, especially when I asked her, "Are we in The Netherlands?"

"Yes," she laughed.

As I walked out, I accidentally walked onto a freshly mopped floor that a girl was mopping directly behind me. I retracted myself and apologized, and the girls working there laughed, as if they thought, "Everything I've heard about Americans is true! They *are* idiots!" It didn't help that I realized that I had to pee, once I got back out to my car with my food. So, I walked back into the Burger King, around the freshly mopped floor, and into the bathroom. As I came out, the girl was mopping another section of floor, and she looked at me like, "Don't walk though this freshly mopped floor." She smiled, either out of pity or approval (I couldn't tell.)

I've been drinking a ton of sparkling water on this trip. I hope it's as hydrating as regular water. Most of the sparkling water in the USA is now associated with the evil corporation, Nestlé. I don't see any Nestlé logos on this sparkling water over here.

I couldn't read the signs, and I expected some kind of border patrols between countries, that's why I asked the girl at Burger King if we were in The Netherlands.

The highways in Germany, The Netherlands, and Belgium are really pretty once you get out of the city, with beautiful farmland and green everywhere.

A 261-mile car drive can be pleasant. Driving 261 miles through New Mexico is usually Heaven on Earth for me. Driving 261 miles between Washington, D.C. and New York is not pleasant. The 261-mile drive from Bremen to Zennegat 13, in

Mechelen, Belgium, was something in-between.

About six hours after leaving the flat, I was on the brink of falling asleep from jet lag, and a bit bloated from Burger King, and hot and humid in the Friday evening rush hour traffic of a town called Mechelen, Belgium. Siri had led me to a dirt road that ran along a canal. I thought it was a bike trail at first, so I scolded Siri, and turned around. In my rearview mirror, I saw a car leaving from it, and realized it was a road, so I turned around, and headed back.

"You'll have to get out of your car and walk the rest of the way. It's 1.5 miles," Siri said.

I was in the mood for a walk at this point. I just wanted to get out of the car and the constant traffic. I could see why that poor weary musician from days of yore concluded to give up looking for Zennegat 13. I didn't feel like driving another two inches/centimeters in that traffic.

I got out of my tiny rental car, and walked along the trail. About a half-mile in, I realized I could totally drive the car on this road (and I should drive. That way, if I find the venue, I'll already have all my equipment with me.) So, I got back into the tiny car, and drove the dirt road toward where I thought Zennegat 13 was supposed to be. The canal on my right was pretty. There were little houseboats docked on the other side. There were dozens and dozens of huge rabbits bumbling about (none of them would let me get close enough to take a photo though.) Lush greenery was everywhere.

I drove a little more than a mile until a sign and a huge pile of lumber stopped me. I got out of my car, and walked around the pile of lumber towards where I thought Zennegat 13 would be. After I walked around the lumber, I could see a building up on my left. I walked toward it, and thankfully, saw a sign that said "Zennegat 13: EETCAFE." I walked into the venue.

"Hello!" No one was there, so I yelled from the bar.

"Hello," a man answered, and walked from the kitchen area

with a smile on his face. "Is this your first show of the tour, or your last?" he asked.

"First," I replied with a big laugh. Either he knew of a Songs and Whispers pattern, or was being funny, or both.

The man was the owner. His name is Yan (I think.) He spoke English well, and he's a really cool guy. No, I mean it. This dude is as cool as the other side of a pillow. Later, when he introduced me to someone, he said, "This is 'Fast Heart Mart' all the way form the US of Fu#%in' A." He told me "zennegat" means, "canal" (I don't remember which language he said.) He immediately poured me Belgium's finest beer, and we talked about the gig. He told me to start about 8:00 p.m., and be done by 10:00 p.m. He recommended I play acoustically, which was fine with me, because I didn't want to lug in all that equipment.

"Is my car ok parked where it is?" I asked.

"The city officials are ok with dumping all that stuff there! Why not dump your car there too?" he replied.

Yan and I laughed some more as another guy walked in and announced that he was going to be on the radio that night, and wanted to promote my show. The man who would be on the radio sounded French. I asked him where he was from and he said, "I'm a true Belgian: my mom is French and my dad is German," or something like that. Then he went on about not believing in countries/nationalities, and that meat is murder, and other issues, including a corrupt beer company to boycott. All his talk was fine at first, but he kept espousing his propaganda all night long, and then it became annoying. All I could think about when I first started talking to him was that chicken sandwich I had eaten earlier at Burger King, but by the end of the night, I wanted to tell him, "You're preaching to the choir." I never got around to it, as I was busy talking to others. His artwork is great, and he seems like a cool guy, but I get the feeling that he's pretty new to all the activist propaganda and is a bit overzealous (he was also a bit overzealous when he clapped along with the beat when I would play music.) It's good though, because on the radio he kept saying things like, "Be a vegan." Some people do still need to hear that.

I went to my car and got ready for the gig. Once ready, I grabbed my huge guitar/banjo bag, and smallish merch/suitcase, and walked the short distance to Zennegat 13.

The people at Zennegat 13 were sweet and kind. They were attentive to my music and me. They smiled a lot as I played. At first, there were probably 10 people in the small room. Then, about 10 more came in while I was playing. It was nice to see that people here were not reluctant to crowd in together, even if they were obviously strangers.

Everyone seemed to enjoy the show, and so did I. I started the show by saying I had traveled 10,000 miles to play this show for them, and that this was my first show ever in Europe. I passed the hat around for each of my two sets, and announced my CDs for sale, and my business cards. I made about €100 (90 from tips and 10 from a CD sale.) That'll be enough to pay for the fuel it took to drive here.

I was surprised how willingly the crowd sang along with me when I asked them. They even sang a Sri Chinmoy chant with me called "Sky Blue Flower," which was a bit challenging for them because their English was not fluent. There was a special moment when I played my song, "Everything's Alright." Everyone was quiet for that song and especially attentive, and they sang the last "Ooooohs" with me.

After the show, Yan brought me some food to eat. Guess what he brought me? Chili sin carne! Ha ha ha ha! I'm fairly certain he had no idea that I've been kind of living off cans of chili sin carne since I arrived to Germany. His chili sin carne was way better though.

It's interesting, once I stopped playing music, most of the people left. Music really does bring people together. Then it was time for bed. I thought it'd be too late to check into the hostel I had booked. Yan offered me a stay on his boat, but I did not want to leave my car and all my gear unattended. I considered sleeping in my huge guitar/banjo bag, but it's not quite that big. So, I slept in my sleeping bag, on a yoga mat that Pi Jacobs gave me, beside my tiny car, outside Zennegat 13, at the End of the Universe.

(Probably the best sleep of the tour yet.)

Day 8: A Naked German Gig

THAT'S RIGHT! I played a show for naked people today (but more on that later.)

Sleeping outside after the Zennegat 13 gig was the right choice. I get the feeling that sleeping outside in Belgium is not often possible, because I think it rains a lot, and is often too cold. However, I had a great sleep on this June night: just my sleeping bag, a yoga mat, and me under the foggy Belgian sky. It drizzled a bit, but that was alright. I only slept like four or five hours, but it was a deep sleep. Also, are there poisonous snakes or spiders in this part of the world? What about mosquitoes? It seems like there would be a ton of mosquitoes, but I didn't experience any.

Call me crazy, but I felt the energy of Van Gogh around there. For me, Van Gogh represents the artist with all the vision and none of the fortune or fame. It's amazing that he hardly sold any of his work while he was alive, but now his paintings are some of the most priceless works of art *ever!* Weird. Just another of Life's many paradoxes.

I awoke surrounded by fog and rabbits. I kind of expected to be a bit hung-over, as I had drunk three of Belgium's finest brews at Zennagat 13. For the most part, I don't drink. Alcoholism runs in my family, and it's also against my Baha'i beliefs. However, when in Belgium… I do as the Belgians (at least for one night.) A lot of times, I wake up with my head feeling foggy, especially if I've had alcohol the night before. However, today the weather was foggy and my head was clear. Fantastic.

Dear Reader,

I have a confession to make: I write these journal entries in the morning, but as though I am writing them at night. I run this deception because it makes the tenses way easier. I am glad that people are enjoying these journal entries. I think writing these has given me some more meaning to my trip. Also, I'm a creative person, and this journal helps me stay sane by fulfilling my creative need while on the road (it's hard for me to write music when anyone else is around, or if I'm uncomfortably hot or cold. I'm much more hardy when it comes to journaling, though.) Thanks for coming along for the ride. I would like to keep writing them; although it takes a lot of time and energy, and I'm not sure I'll be able to do it. It's been tricky deciding what's appropriate to include in this journal for the whole world to read. One aspect is for sure, I will not write about my romantic life.

Thanks to my high school creative writing teacher, Beth Pollock, for teaching me to keep a journal in high school. I've been doing it for years, and it's coming in handy right now. Beth Pollock had a sign in her class that said, "How do I know what I think unless I see what I say?" Writing is a powerful tool.

I looked around the town of Mechelen, Belgium a bit in the early morning fog. Not many people were awake until about 8:00 a.m., and even then there weren't many out and about. It was a great time to explore because there wasn't any traffic. I drove down the wrong way on one-way streets and no one even knew it! Then I wrote the journal entry "Zennegat 13: The Gig at the End of the Universe!"

I hit the road at about noon to head back to Germany, and a town called *Oldenburg*, for a show I would be playing for naked people. I felt like I had pulled one over on The System by sleeping outside the night before. I didn't have to pay a hotel/hostel. I didn't have to accept the good will of someone to let me stay at their place. I just went to sleep on the ground, woke up, and carried on with Life - except, I stepped in dog shit when I woke up! I thought I had cleaned it all off of my shoe, but my car still stank of it. That's when I noticed it was on my pant leg! Ewwwww! I pulled over at a gas station and cleaned it up. This gas station had a turnstile! To enter the bathroom you were supposed to pay! What the...? That felt like too much to me. I snuck through the turnstile thinking, "If someone stops me I'm going to go pee on their lawn." What the heck? When will the day come when they try and charge us for blinking? (Cue Nathan Payne's song "Living in the Drunk Tank of My Dreams," when he sings, *"What's the cost of getting lost?/ What's the fine for feeling fine?/ What's the tax if I relax?/ Oh, I don't know man, I'm just waitin' for a train..."*) I've been told that Germans are very into rules. I get it. I like rules too, but paying for a bathroom? That's going too far. Would it work in the USA?

Now, back on the Autobahn, I find myself fascinated by these roads. How is it that Germans can be so into rules, but have an Autobahn that lets anyone go as fast as they want? My dad always had sports cars when I was growing up (Corvettes, Mustangs, Chevelles, etc.) I always found it odd, why a person would have such a fast car if they weren't allowed to drive it fast? The Autobahn would be the perfect solution. I wish I had a fast car for my stay in Germany. I mean, I don't really desire a sports car of my own, but I'd like to try it sometime. The Toyota

Yaris I've rented is too dangerous to drive fast. It's one thing to go 180 mph in a Mercedes Benz, but it's a completely different thing to go even 100 mph in a Toyota, Yaris. Sports cars are made for speed. They are usually wider for stability, have speed-tuned suspensions, and tires rated for high speed... The list goes on. Though I'd like to floor it in my Toyota, Yaris rental, I keep my speed reasonable and prudent for the well being of everyone involved. It'd be great to see my dad in a Corvette over here though. He could go as fast he wanted!

I see amazing things on the Autobahn. I saw the river Rhein today. It was pretty high; its banks up to the trees beside it, flooding the forest floor (I've heard Paris is flooded too.) I also saw a four-wheeler on the Autobahn! What the heck? It was like a "Mad Max" movie seeing that guy out there on the Autobahn going 110-120 kph! Wow! That's gotta be dangerous. (I know I fluctuated between mph and kph, but I have to write about high speeds in mph as kph don't have the same weight to me (even though I think the metric system is far superior, and we should adopt it all over the world, including the USA.)

As I drove, I had thoughts about my Life's Path. What's gonna happen to me now? I'm 39 years old. I've quit my great day job as the videographer and musician of the great company Pilgrimage of the Heart Yoga studio. The house I was trying to buy in Joshua Tree doesn't seem to be happening. I'm not sure how much money I'll make on this tour. All these thoughts came into my brain as I drove, but I'm wise enough now not to let them win. I resolved the negative thoughts by realizing that *Life is happening.* I'm healthy and alive. I did a great job at the Pilgrimage of the Heart, and it was time for me to take a break. The house in Joshua Tree wasn't meant to be, and I did my best to buy it. I have a great affordable apartment in San Diego, with a great landlord who likes me (and who has told me that he wouldn't mind if I stayed another 30 years.) In a lot of ways, I'm living my dream. It's not exactly as I had imagined, but what is?

Would Life be as magical if we got exactly what we wanted all the time?

I arrived to the naked gig in Oldenburg, Germany. I was imagining it was going to be at a hippie nudist colony, but it was at a section of a big public recreation center. My liaison (is this the right word?) Arne, from Songs and Whispers, met me there to assist me with the gig. We carried all the musical equipment inside. We were fully clothed, and just about everyone else was naked.

I have respect for nudists. They are doing their thing. I think I understand their plight. Clothes can segregate human beings. Without our clothes, we all do look much more similar. Much more equal. Nudity is honesty. I'm into honesty, a lot.

Arne and I set up the stage and then hung out waiting for show time. We talked about life in general. His native language is German, but he speaks English well. We mentioned in our conversation the notion of money in the music business.

"It takes billions to be a millionaire in the music business," Arne joked. (Ha! I'd never heard that one before.)

"We all know money is not real anymore," I said. "It's not backed by gold. What is real, is music bringing people together. Like last night at Zennagat 13 - the place was empty as soon as I stopped playing. Whether those people liked my particular music doesn't matter. We all came together for a moment and had a smile, and other feelings, together. That's real," I said. Arne agreed.

Arne is very intelligent, and my respect for him, and Songs and Whispers, is growing as this tour goes. Songs and Whispers is doing something, and it's kind of interesting to see. I'm not quite sure if the experiment will benefit the artists, but I do believe Songs and Whispers has the right intention. In this world of constant flux, no one knows what's going to work anymore. All the models are shattered. We have to create new ones. If we follow old models, we will usually fall short of our goals. We have to listen to our intuition, and see what happens. Songs and Whispers seems to be trying to help the arts in Germany, and across the world. Let's see what happens.

Playing for naked people was an experience, for sure. But, when it came time to play, the sun was going down. Most of the people just lingered far away from where I played. The ones who sat up close to me to listen, covered themselves in towels, probably to keep themselves warm, and perhaps to be a bit discreet. It was a fun performance, and I would do it again without hesitation.

I came back to the artist flat in Bremen. The Australian Crew was hanging out at the kitchen table. They are inviting, kind, and generous people, and we talked about our tour so far. Their accents are great (especially Ripley's.) They had a gig all day today! Getting to their gig yesterday was only supposed to take two hours, but it took four and a half hours because traffic was so bad. Otherwise, they are happy to be here (just like me.)

Tonight, I met the final musicians on the tour, Brian Laidlaw and his wife, Ashley. I listened to Brian's music before I came on the tour, and I'm really impressed. After meeting those two, I went to bed, exhausted.

Day off tomorrow!

Day 8.5: The Real World - Bremen

(Me, Ripley, Georgina, Brian, Ashley, and Danny)

REMEMBER the reality show on MTV called "The Real World?" I woke up this morning wondering if I had inadvertently been cast onto a new season of that show, somehow. My Australian rock star roommate, Ripley, was snoring, as his cell phone played a quiet alarm of a whistling flute. The combination of which sounded like a small freight train preparing at the station. Ripley, if you read this, please know that I think you're great, and fun, and talented, and one of the coolest people I've ever met. Ripley is a great guy. A character. It's Life. These things happen, and I know Ripley did not mean for it to happen. As I'm pretty sure I was already awake, the snoring did not awaken me. I'm usually awake with the sun every day. It was just a reality check. There are now six of us artists (on a continent foreign to us all) living in the three rooms of this apartment: one narrow bathroom; a smallish kitchen; a medium length hallway; and no living room. Even though everyone seems really accommodating and considerate, this could get interesting.

I've been living alone for almost three years now. I can use the bathroom anytime I want. I can have a private phone conversation anytime I want. I can change my clothes anytime I want. I'm not against the idea of a chamber pot. Why did the world abandon them? They'd come in handy at times like these. This situation we are all in is a trip. Makes me wonder if we are part a Songs and Whispers experiment sometimes. So far, it's a fun experiment.

Brian and Ashley left to play a show at a local street fair. The Australians (is it ok to refer to you as "The Australians," "Aussies," or "Georgina's Crew?" I need a succinct name) and I sat in the kitchen talking. We talked about the music business. Somehow we got on the subject of Nirvana.

"Do you like Nirvana and the Grunge Movement?" Georgina asked.

"Heck yeah," I answered. This was another reality check for me. I was 12 years old when Nirvana hit the mainstream. My ninth grade math teacher told my high school class about Nirvana, before anyone had ever heard of them.

"Have you kids ever heard of this band Naveena?" Mr. Hoffman asked.

"No, Mr. Hoffman, we're not impressed that you know of this band that no one has heard. Just get back to teaching," we surly teenagers replied.

"Well, I used to teach their drummer, David Grohl. I hear his band is supposed to be the next big thing."

We teenaged kids didn't think anything of it, until about three weeks later, when the "Smells Like Teen Spirit" video came on MTV and changed the world forever!

My ninth grade math teacher was also Dave Grohl's math teacher. I have walked around the world ever since, thinking that I was part of the original Grunge Movement. I had long hair from the time I was 12, until about age 34. This conversation made me realize that that's not obvious to the rest of the world anymore.

Georgina told me, during this conversation, that Ripley thinks I look like Michael J. Fox. Ripley meant no offense, and I took none. It's not the first time I've heard this. I'm flattered, because I like Michael J. Fox. He seems like a cool guy. He was a teenage heartthrob, and I love his acting work, especially "Back to the Future." However, Michael J. Fox is not a rock star. Michael J. Fox is as bland as vanilla ice cream. Is that what I've become? Bland, like vanilla ice cream? How did I get this way? I want to grow all my hair back right now to cover my eyes. I'm an eccentric rock star and I want the world to know it, as soon as I enter the door.

Maybe my anti-style is cool? One of my favorite current/living/relevant rock stars today is Isaac Brock of Modest Mouse and he doesn't look particularly eccentric. He kind of looks bland, but he's great, and I like his understated style. Mark Kozelek (Red House Painters, Sun Kil Moon, solo) is also one of my favorite rock stars, and he also has a Michael J Fox, bland vanilla look. But his songs are some of my favorites, and I think his work is some of the most legit, relevant art in the world today. It was another reality check that the rest of the world might perceive me as being vanilla ice cream. Inside, I feel like rainbow sherbet mixed with Rocky Road.

I had the day off from playing music today. I don't think I'll have another day off for a while, so I did my laundry, and caught up on some other things. I didn't know where the washing machine was, so I washed my clothes in the bathtub with liquid body wash. Washing jeans in a bathtub is not easy. I dried my clothes in my car. What better place to dry clothes than a hot car on a beautiful summer day? The grocery stores are closed here on

Sundays, which is kind of cool. Giving the workers a break!

We all went to dinner tonight at a great restaurant called "Haus am Walde," but we couldn't read the menu. Ashley had this cool Google translate app on her cell phone that allows her to point her phone camera at the menu, and the words come up translated into English! Holy Mackrel! The future is now! We fussed with the menu for a while, and then the waiter came and said in his best English, "I have an English menu for Englishmen." Georgina pointed out a vegan meal, and I ate that (carrots, parsnips, pilaf, and other vegetables, in a curry sauce.) Nice. We all shared stories of making money in today's Armageddon music business.

It was a beautiful summer night in Bremen, Germany. I'm not sure what the world thinks of my style, my music, or me, but at least I'm able to see the rest of the world like this! Pretty cool, man.

(P.S. I miscounted a day somewhere, so today is 8.5 to get back on track.)

Day 9: Living The Dream?

(Photo by Georgina on the way to the grocery store)

STARTED OFF the events for today by attending the Songs and Whispers weekly artist meeting. This is a meeting that will happen every Monday to discuss the shows, and any other questions about the tour. An intern from China also came to the meeting. Wow! She has to speak three languages: English, German, *and* her native Chinese. I've always had respect for someone who can move to a foreign country, and live in a land where they have to learn a completely new language and culture, but now I have even more.

Georgina, Ripley, and I walked to the grocery store together. We would look at all the different things for sale, and I'd ask, "Do y'all have this product in Australia?" Then they'd ask, "Do you have this in America?" We all helped each other find stuff.

It's starting to feel more natural to go to the grocery store now. I'm getting used to not being able to instantly read things.

On the walk to the grocery store, Georgina wanted to take a photo of me lying in some white flowers. I lay down and let her take the photo. The flowers were pretty, but as I lay there, I thought, "How much of these flowers and grass is covered in dog excrement and how much is really pure like we'd like to believe?"

The other day, at the nude sauna, every one of the Christmas lights burned out in my Fast Heart Mart sign. I think there's too much current in the German electrical system. I decided to go to a hardware store to replace them. It's been perfect weather here so far, but on the way, a gigantic rainstorm occurred (which was nice, because it was really hot and sunny before that.) It was raining so hard against my car roof that I almost wanted to put in earplugs, because it was so loud. I thought Noah might come save me in his ark at any minute.

I only went the wrong way down a one-way street once on this trip, despite the torrential rain. I found some great LED lights for my sign! The hardware store looked like any Home Depot in the USA, except it was more organized and easier to find assistance.

Then I went to perform my show at a venue called "Falstaff" in Bremen. Georgina and Ripley were sharing the bill with me.

Falstaff is an intimate theatre-type stage within a bar/restaurant, within an art center, in Bremen.

I'm still figuring out how much of my stage banter to use here in Germany. Stage banter is a big part of my show. However, I speak in English, and I'm still determining how much of it the German audiences will appreciate. I've decided to just do my thing as if they all speak English. I'll usually throw as much German in there as I can, but for the most part, I just gotta be myself (and so far it's going over pretty well.) I find that a lot of people may not speak English, but almost all of them understand it. People also really enjoy singing and clapping along when I prompt them.

The audience showed up right on time. There were probably about 30 people at this performance. It went well. Made some money. Sold some CDs. Made some new fans. I could tell by the audience's faces that they enjoyed themselves. Georgina and Ripley liked my set. Georgina said it made her cry.

I was impressed with Georgina and Ripley's performance! They put a lot of energy out! Georgina's songs are good, and her stage presence is excellent. Ripley's a great guitar player and singer. At one point in their set, they did a medley of cover songs that was the most all-encompassing and variant medley I've ever heard. They give me the feeling that Australia is a great place for music these days, because their enthusiasm is contagious. The Australian Crew is growing on me by leaps and bounds. It can be hard to get a word in edgewise with them sometimes, but I'm realizing that sharing their experiences is their way of caring. Their enthusiasm and consideration are unstoppable.

I drove home tonight pondering what some of my friends back in the USA have been telling me.

"You're living the dream," they say. It's a nice reminder, but sometimes I doubt that I *am* living the dream. I'm a 39-year-old unmarried musician playing for audiences that have never heard of me before (and may not be able to understand me), and getting paid way less than minimum wage. I have no job to go back to after the European trip is over. No ties to any place. No clear future. Are these flowers covered with dog excrement or are they as pure as we'd like to believe?

Then, a profound thought occurred to me: maybe when Life puts you in a place where you can only live in the moment (because the future is uncertain and the past is irrelevant), you *are* living the dream? When Life forces you to be present and grateful for all that you have in the current moment, yet there is no other place you'd rather be, then are you living the dream?

This German tour is what I wanted to do, and I'm doing it. I'm healthy. I have enough money to live. I'm pretty happy. I'm alive, and I'm playing my music for attentive, appreciative audiences.

It's not always glorious, but I'm doing it. I'm living *my* dream, one moment at a time.

Day 10: A TV Show, A Concert & A Boatload O' Booty

IT'S BEEN A HUGE DAY here in Germany! Woke up and had to catch up on some bills from my life back in the USA. Yay! I have just enough to pay my bills! I just needed to figure out a way to pay my van payment for the month, as the bank doesn't accept deposits from outside the USA. I figured it out though. Money is running a bit tight, but I have faith.

Drove to a local TV station, with all of the Songs and Whispers artists, where we recorded a song and an interview. It was fun. The host, Mark, was pleasant. I could tell he did his research before we arrived, which is always impressive. He had heard of Danny's band from the 80's with their song "Send Me An Angel," and I thought that was impressive too. He told me that he'd traveled twice to the USA (each time for a two-month trip), and that he liked it.

I performed my song "I'm An Alien and I Want to Go Home." If I could only pick one song to represent me, I feel like that one represents me the most. I pointed out to Mark that I think the song is about how human beings have devolved in a lot of ways. I don't understand why we've allowed ourselves to get this far off course: working so much; stressed out; isolated; and neglecting the most important things in Life, such as love for each other. I even told him about the Baha'i faith when he asked if I'm religious (http://www.bahai.org).

Doing this TV show (and being on this tour in general) is inspiriting me to look at myself as an artist and what it is I represent. I think I've had a lot of variety in my songwriting, but I think what people want is one song that sounds great and other songs that sound similar to that masterpiece. Have I created my masterpiece yet? Will I ever? Hmmm... good things to ponder.

I had to leave the station quickly, as I had to drive an hour away to a town called *Fährstraße* to a venue called *"Weserperle."* It was tricky to find at first, because it was hidden by a hill. I knocked on a random house door. The woman was friendly, but only spoke German, and pointed me in the right direction. Once over the hill, I saw the river, and eventually found Weserperle.

Weserperle is sort of a cafe on the Weser River. It sells food and drinks, and alcohol. The women who run it are sweet. They even have vegan food there, and I ate a vegan burger, French fries, and a vegan slice of pie! (Note: Even though all the artists are working for tips at all the shows, we seem to be getting fed dinner everywhere we go. This is nice because the food is usually very good, and we save money.)

I was booked to play at 6:00 p.m. (18:00 hours.) I had just enough time to set up, and take a 15-minute break, before I had to hit the stage. It was one of those days when each event leads directly into the next.

The shows on the tour so far have all started on time, which is good, because just about everyone shows up on time. It's fun to watch. Twenty minutes before the show starts, there may not be anyone. However, five minutes before the show starts, if anyone is going to come, then most of them will be there! I love it.

The performance went well. Only one little girl plugged her ears when I played. Sometimes kids do that because they're brats. Sometimes I really am not sounding good. I opened by telling them, "I'm Fast Heart Mart, from San Diego, California, and I drove all the way here to play for you." They didn't think it was all that funny. I said a few more small things to break the ice, but I still didn't feel like I had penetrated into their hearts. I like to warm up an audience and make them feel comfortable, so they'll open up and enjoy themselves more.

"*Moin*," I said. As far as I can understand, moin is a Northern German dialect for "Hello, how are you?" Arne told me about this word the first day I arrived, and each time I've said it to a local German it brings a smile to their face. It definitely brought smiles to the faces in this audience at Weserperle!

Sometimes, I think it's as if the German audiences are only interested in the music, and not me, the artist. They are interested in the magic, not the vessel in which it is delivered to this Earthly plane. I am absolutely cool with that. I love that, actually!

I played two 45-minute sets for the crowd. It was an absolutely gorgeous day on the waterfront there. It had been hot and humid around Bremen when I left, but out at the riverside the weather was perfect!

There were probably 100-150 people in the audience, strewn along the riverside. I think they liked my music because they were respectful and attentive, clapping enthusiastically after each song. They smiled at me, and tipped me well when I'd pass the hat around. They even bought CDs.

I'm still getting a feeling for what they like around these parts. Overall, my song "Everything's Alright," seems to be the one they like the most. Before I came to Germany, I thought Europeans would gravitate towards the faster banjo songs, because those songs are something they probably don't get much of around here. But I'm finding they like slow songs just as much when peppered in amongst the fast ones. I hope to figure it out soon.

During the first set, I saw a woman in the audience who seemed particularly enthusiastic about my music. So, during the break between set one and set two, I asked if she'd like to take some photos for me. She did, and she took some good ones! Thank you, Gaby! Gaby spoke her best English to communicate with me, and I spoke my best German. It was cool.

I was fortunate to have such beautiful weather out on the riverside today, and I knew it. I could imagine it getting pretty cold, rainy and windy around here. After the show, a woman at the cafe told me that last year, five of these concerts were rained out! I told the audience what a beautiful day I thought it was, and they all smiled. Then I told them, "I live in San Diego, California and it's like this almost every day there!" They laughed. One guy was taking photographs. He reminded me of Josh Lubbers, my good friend from high school. He especially reminded me of Josh when he immediately flipped me off for saying it's beautiful like this almost everyday where I live in San Diego, CA. Ha!

There are events like this back in the USA, but somehow I never get invited. I also don't apply. It made me think I should start applying. I usually don't apply, because I assume no one will like me (it'd be like having Bjork play at Disney World or something.)

After the show, I collected all my tips out of my hat. Holy Mackrel! There must have been 20 pounds of change! Before I drove home, I counted it all. (I've decided to stop divulging to the world how much money I'm making on each of the shows, as I think it's tacky.) Suffice to say, I left the Weser riverside feeling like a pirate who had finally found his lost booty - ready to sail away on the Weser River with my boatload of money! Arrrr!

(Playing Weserperle, a cafe on the Weser River)

Day 11: Meet The Münsters

Q: WHAT do you call trendy people who gentrify new colonies on The Moon?
A: Münsters. (Get it? Moonsters? Hipsters/Münsters?)

I had to write an invoice to Songs and Whispers and get some groceries before I left the artist flat in Bremen. Ripley helped me write out my invoice. Ripley is a professional musician all the way, even down to invoicing his jobs. Ripley is one of the kindest and most considerate people I have ever met. Whenever someone makes a mistake with Ripley (such as knocking on the door to the bathroom when he's already in there), the person may say, "I'm sorry," and Ripley will reply, "All good," in the most compassionate Australian accent ever. What a sweetheart.

I have been eating lots of cherries since I arrived in Germany last week. I love cherries! It's cherry season in the Northern

Hemisphere. Alas, the grocery store seems to be running out of cherries now. I hope cherry season isn't over already.

I try to eat fruit for breakfast every day. I have a few friends in San Diego who are raw vegans, and they have been influencing me. They say that you can eat as much whole fruit as you'd like by itself (because it's not fruit sugar that causes high blood sugar levels in the body, it's eating fruit sugar *with fats* that causes problems.) Fat slows the absorption rate in the body by coating the cell walls and causing the sugars to stay unabsorbed in the blood. Fruit is high in vitamins and minerals that the human body needs. Therefore, I eat as much fruit as I can for breakfast. (There. I wrote about my breakfast routine.)

I'm feeling more comfortable at the grocery store. I can find my way around much better now. One thing I've noticed though, is that people treat the checkout lane like they do the Autobahn: tailgating my food on the conveyor belt. Then, when I'm done paying, and go to bag my own groceries, people are tailgating their food right up against mine. Like this woman did to me today! I think the woman knew I didn't speak German, and took it as a sign of weakness (or inferiority) and decided to prey upon the weak. I have a sense of humor about it, but sometimes I want to motion and say, "Back up lady! Give me some room here! I've gotta bag my food. I don't want your food ending up in my bags."

I drove on the Autobahn to *Münster*, Germany today for my show at *"Frauenstraße 24."* I saw a Ford, Mustang flying past me in the fast lane!

Münster is a beautiful city with old architecture and narrow streets, and bicyclists are everywhere. I've seen some pretty women here in Germany, but not as many as I saw in Münster today. Holy Mackrel! It was like super models were everywhere, riding their bicycles to the university on the cobblestone streets with their long flowing hair waving in the beautiful June air. Wow!

The people at Frauenstraße 24 were super friendly. The owner is a man named Jürgen, and he personally assisted me with my concert there. He speaks English pretty well. We spoke before the show about a lot of different things. He likes Tom Waits, Bob Dylan, Neil Young, etc. I thanked him for having music in this Post-Apocalyptic Armageddon Digital-Music Age.

I was humbled by how accommodating people were to speak English to me there (and everywhere in Germany), even if they feel like their English is not very good. Thank you, Germany! Earlier today, my artist flat mates and I met a man who has a radio show. The man said he liked the way the Australians spoke English, but that people from the USA spoke too fast. Dang! I wonder if people can understand me? Do I talk too fast? I know I mumble quite a bit. Hmmm... Sometimes, when I'm speaking to people who don't speak English very well, I catch myself just speaking to them louder (as if they can't hear me), but I don't think that's very effective.

The show was mellow. Only a few people were randomly there, but they were respectful and attentive, and they smiled and clapped, and tipped relatively well. If people didn't clap, I'd say *"Danke,"* until they did (prompting them to realize the song was over.) Saying "moin," did not work well here. Apparently, it's more of a Northern Germany thing.

Some of the shows on the Songs and Whispers circuit have been happening for a long time, and there are people who come regularly. This show at Frauenstraße 24 in Münster has only been on the circuit for about six months, so it's still building up a reputation. It's a lovely room, and it would have probably had more people if the weather weren't so dang nice! Funny, last night I was thankful for the great weather, and tonight the great weather stifled me. I still made enough from tips and CD sales to pay for my gas, and a little more left over. Cool!

Playing shows that are not very well attended reminds me of the stories my dad used to tell me, when I was growing up in

Virginia, about bluegrass musicians he used to go see in the 60's, 70's, and early 80's. "I went and saw Don Reno at a Pizza Hut once. There was hardly anyone there, but he didn't care. He still played his heart out and was happy to be playing music." Those stories my dad would tell me inspired me to want to be a musician. Here I am, livin' the dream.

Jürgen bought some of my many pounds of change. Now I have a huge wallet full of bills! This is another uncouth thought, especially since I've seriously never been to a strip club, nor had the desire, but what do strippers get for tips here? Are there strippers here in Germany? If so, do people throw one and two Euro coins at them or is it a €5 paper bill minimum? Do the strippers have to carry a bucket around with them for all the change? I think I'm just wondering because it can get cumbersome really quickly.

I drove home late into the night. I'm not sure if I got a ticket on the Autobahn when I saw a red light flash. I may have been driving too fast on a particular stretch. Are there speed cameras on the Autobahn? Leave it to me to get a speeding ticket on the Autobahn! I've never had a speeding ticket in my entire life until I drove on the Autobahn! Oh, the irony.

Another concern is that my data on my cell phone is getting eaten alive by all this GPS usage. I received a text message today saying I'm gonna be charged $50 for my extra data usage, and I've only been here for a week! I've gotta start using a paper map!

Q: What do you call scary creatures on The Moon?

A: Münsters! Ha! I'll be here in Germany for the rest of this month folks.

Gute Nacht!

Day 12: Tillmann Hahn's Gasthaus

(There's a beach in Germany on the Baltic Sea!)

I HAD A FOUR-HOUR DRIVE to my show tonight in the northernmost part of Germany on the Baltic Sea. My show was at a venue called *"Tillmann Hahn's Gasthaus,"* on *Ostseeallee* 2, 18225 in *Kühlungsborn,* Germany. The drive there was pretty, especially the closer I came to the venue. Rolling green hills with tree lined roads, wild flowers and cornfields. I wondered about the cornfields. Isn't corn originally from the Americas? Is Germany now growing genetically modified corn in surplus like the USA and experiencing all the corruption that surrounds this crop? Hmmm. Who knows?

I arrived in Ostseeallee at about 3:30 p.m. (15:30), and parked. I wrestled with the parking meter for a bit, doing my best to provide it €3 worth of my smallest coins. The €0.50 coins were the smallest it would take, so I made sure to give the machine those. I'm still trying to unload some of my heavy coins, from all the tips that are occupying the cup holders in my car.

Ostseeallee appeared to be a tourist town. Lots of old, retired people walked the streets. I reluctantly write the word "old," as I don't want to sound disrespectful. I think age should be respected as long as it has wisdom to back it up. I usually assume an older person is wise until they prove otherwise by saying or doing something that leads me to believe that they are fearful, status-quo-dwelling people who have not learned a thing except for how to shut up and make money at any expense. As I drove through Ostseeallee, I began to dread that these tourists walking around were not wise old people, but people who would hear my music tonight, and scoff at such nonsense.

I used to do some busking (musical street performance) in Old Town in Santa Fe, New Mexico and Old Town in Albuquerque. A lot of times, playing for the tourists there was a drag. They were people on vacation that wanted to meet Georgia O'Keefe. I love Georgia O'Keefe! She's had a huge influence on me as a dedicated artist. However, Georgia O'Keefe has been gone since the late 80's when she passed away at the old age of 99. I think Georgia O'Keefe was a wise old lady. The tourists were disappointed to see me out there instead, singing about the irony of the democracy of the USA being built upon the genocide of the indigenous peoples of the land. I'd sing a song called "Richman," about a rich man who gives away most of his wealth because he realizes he'll never be able to spend it all in his life time, and that to give it all to his children would only create more people with entitlement issues in the world.

I looked around Ostseeallee and saw a bunch of older tourists, and cringed. I asked myself, as I have many times before, "Does this venue I'm going to be playing at tonight know who I am and what I'm about? Is everyone going to flee in terror at the sound of me?"

I walked into Tillmann Hahn's Gasthaus. It was super fancy on the outside. It looked like a five star hotel, maybe even a six or seven star hotel. I asked the woman at the reception counter, "Do you speak English?" because I still have not perfected my *"Sprichst du Englisch?"* The woman simply answered, "No," and did not seem at all interested in helping me any further, as she turned away. I thought to myself for a minute, then said, *"Ich bin musician... musica,"* as I played air guitar. That worked. She instantly understood what needed to happen. She directed me to a back office to introduce me to Tillman, the owner of the restaurant where I'd be playing.

Tillman is a big man, about six-feet three inches tall and 250 pounds. He speaks English well, though he's German. As he showed me around the venue, we talked about how things would go. Tillman is a chef who opened this fancy restaurant four years ago. I quickly realized that he is as calm (and calming) as a cup of chamomile tea.

"We want you to play this show tonight as if it were a concert. We don't want you to be background music," Tillman told me. Wow! This guy was speaking my language, especially when he started talking about the role of the artist in today's world.

"Are you an artist?" I asked Tillman, alluding to the fact that he is a chef.

"I am a craftsman," he answered.

"What's the difference?" I asked him.

"Craftsmen are more practical. I create to serve people. Artists... artists are not really living in this world. Artists are motivated by something beyond this world," Tillman answered.

I could have cried tears of joy at his answer. All my fears and doubts about the tourists that may come to the show tonight were dissolved like sugar into tea. Tillman knew exactly what he was getting into by having authentic artists at his fancy restaurant. I did not need to worry about offending his fine diners. I was expected to be myself. Hallelujah!

It turns out that Tillman has published three books on cooking. His restaurant is fancy, with a healthy dose of authenticity. I'm impressed by this man and the conversations we had about veganism, money, artists, and happiness. It's wonderful to know that people like Tillman exist in the world.

As I set up my equipment to play, Modest Mouse's "Third Planet" came on the stereo. Dang! I took it as a sign that I was in the right place at the right time. I love Modest Mouse and what they mean to me: a band that's been out there in the world performing their music since 1993; unknown for a long time, now accepted all over the world as a band to put on the stereo.

The show went alright. There weren't many people there. Tillman says he thinks it's because people are getting ready for their holidays. Apparently, Germany has 13 different summer holiday schedules set up for its citizens. I'm not sure what a holiday schedule is, but I assume it's something similar to a vacation. The people who were there were busy eating their meals. A few people looked up and smiled enthusiastically at me, but for the most part people seemed preoccupied. They did clap at the end of each song. The second set had more people who came just for the music, but still not a whole lot of people were there. Nonetheless, I made enough money to pay for the fuel and have some left over for myself.

Isn't Life funny? The people who stay in the status quo, and take vacations in far away destinations, were the only ones hearing me play my rebellious, unfamiliar songs. Ha! (Another conundrum indeed.) It was interesting to see the couples who may have been married for a long time, living according to how society wanted them to, sitting across from each other at a dinner, on vacation, with nothing to speak of. Then there's the people who are alive and smiling at me, because they recognized that I too am questioning this reality and laughing. They clapped and sang along with me tonight and made the show much more beautiful.

After the show, a couple sitting at a table asked me to join them. They spoke a little bit of English. They were a happily married couple in their 50's, who proudly told me that they have four children. The man told me that he likes to drive 150 mph on the Autobahn. The couple was as sweet as Tillman's chocolates in his bistro, and they were trying hard to connect with me. They even offered me a drink, but I politely declined, as I wanted to take care of myself and stay alert. The language barrier was too much for me though, and I felt frustrated communicating with them, because I was too tired for any tolerance.

Another man came up to me a little while later. He was dressed like he had just come from a country club, covered in white pants and a pastel sweater. He realized quickly that I don't speak German, and said, "You are in Germany, you should speak German," then went on and on about something else. I wanted to tell him to please stop talking. Instead, I just walked away between his thoughts.

When I play a show, *that* is me connecting with the world. Usually, after a show is the worst time to talk to me. I'm drained, and tired, and all talked out.

I spent the night in Tillman's guest room at his personal house.

Day 13: Getting In The Groove At Schwarzer Hermann

I DROVE BACK to Bremen from Ostseeallee, Kühlungsborn, Germany at the Baltic Sea this morning. I listened to "Cut the Cord Radio" as I drove. Cut the Cord Radio is a podcast created by Tyler Mathews in Richmond, Virginia. Tyler Mathews went to the same high school as me in Manassas Park, Virginia. Some mutual friends of ours introduced me to his show. It was nice listening to Cut the Cord Radio on the drive, because I've been having doubts about this journal lately, and those guys on that podcast are being themselves and it's great. I may not agree with everything they say on the show, but I like the show and what it means to me. I find the show very funny at times. It made me feel at home today. (http://www.cutthecordradio.com)

I arrived back in Bremen at 1:30 p.m., just in time to check in for my show at *"Schwarzer Hermann."* However, the check-in time was rescheduled to 6:15 p.m., so I went back to the artist flat, and took a shower, and did some writing.

Honestly, I was feeling pretty ambivalent about Life at this point. Being on the road is great, but I was feeling a bit weary and lonely. I saw a picture of Bob Dylan playing a concert recently, and thought to myself, "What keeps this guy motivated after all these years? Why does he keep getting up on stage, and playing for people? What keeps him from being a total recluse?" The answer is: Bob Dylan does not drive around in parts of the world where he in unknown in a tiny car to play for people who've never heard him. Bob Dylan just gets on the bus and the rest is provided for him. Bob Dylan is great! I love him, don't get me wrong, but he doesn't tour like me. Bob Dylan did some hard travelin' in his early days, sure. But for most of his life, he's had a tour bus, with a driver, and a manager, and a handler, and an agent, and the fame, and the money, etc. Bob Dylan keeps going because he can. He's gone through many phases in his life, and I think he's pretty reclusive.

I went through the motions, and drove myself to Schwarzer Hermann. I have to admit, I'm not used to playing this many consecutive shows anymore (or having to meet this many new club owners every night), so when I showed up to Schwarzer Hermann, I was feeling pretty nonchalant about playing. Schwarzer Hermann is a bar, and I'm not thrilled about bars at this point in my life. People usually go to bars to drink, and scream at their friends, and watch a variety of sports on all the big screens scattered throughout the bar, not to listen to music. Music can be on the stereo now.

I got out of my car, and walked up to Schwarzer Hermann. I saw two men out front setting up some huge TV screens, but I didn't want to bother them. So, I walked into the bar, and introduced myself to the bartender. His name was Sam. Sam is a pleasant guy who was excited that I had arrived. Sam's English was good. He told me where to set up and when I would play. He told me that one of the guys setting up the big screens out front was the owner. Some people might have then gone over to the owner and introduced themselves, but I was not in the mood. I assumed he was busy, and decided to load in all my gear.

As I was preparing for my 7:30 to 9:30 p.m. (19:30-21:30) show, I saw the owner walk by a few times. We still did not make introductions. It wasn't until I started setting up my blue rope of LED lights that the owner spoke.

"Yuck, those are horrible," was the first thing the owner of

Schwarzer Hermann said to me.

"Are you kidding? Do you want me to take them down?" I asked, trying to stay as unattached to this situation as I could.

"No, it's fine I guess," he responded with a slight smile.

At 7:30 p.m., I got up on stage and started to play. There were about nine people in the bar at this point, including the bar tenders. Apparently, this was to be the first night of the soccer world championship games or something, so the owner told me they weren't sure what to expect that night as far as attendance. With only nine people in the bar, I decided to start out my set mellow - background music. My theory is, "if I don't disturb people with volume, I'm halfway to getting them to tolerate my music. Then, I have a chance to pierce their hearts by picking the right songs at the right time."

I started out with an old song of mine called "Desert Dessert." I played it very mellow and sang it even mellower. It went over really well! Everyone in the bar clapped and looked at me with a smile when I was done. I did the next eight songs in the same mellow fashion, and got the same response. I started to think to myself that maybe I should sing and play like this all the time? Rerecord all my songs this way?

A group of women off to my left clapped to the beat. The group started out as three, and grew to five or six as the night went on. They were really into my music!

Overall, it was a pleasant and good night at Schwarzer Hermann. By the end of the night, there were about 35 people in the bar, and it felt like a bona fide concert. I'm not sure what the name "Schwarzer Hermann" means, but I wonder if it has something to do with cigarettes, because all the photos they have inside are of celebrities smoking cigarettes. There are definitely way more smokers here in Germany than I'm used to.

Sam, the bartender, was very accommodating, taking photos for me and serving me some chili CON carne and a beer afterwards. The owner seemed cool as we got to know each other more. I can respect someone not putting on a polite act. Maybe the owner just likes to keep it real, and I'm cool with that! Fortunately for me it was a chilly evening, so most people chose to come inside to hang out. The owner told me that the venue doesn't have permission to have music outside anymore. There was a pleasant man named Johanas (Yohan?) about 27 years old, who sat in front for my second set listening intently. I made some tip money, sold some CDs, and passed out a lot of business cards. I felt in the groove as a traveling musician. This tour has been a bit ambivalent and lonely today, but still there's no other place I'd rather be.

Day 14: Diaries Are Dangerous

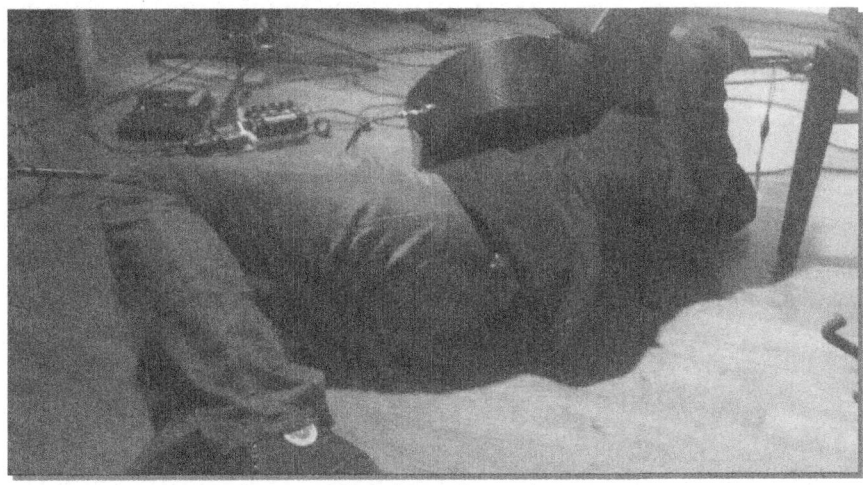

(Punk rock star)

I'VE KEPT a diary/journal for a long time now. I find it helps me to sort out my thoughts and make sense of the world. It helps me to make Life more enjoyable, because it makes Life into a story. However, my journals have gotten me in trouble over the years. It's a dangerous thing to write down your thoughts, in the chance that another person may read something you've written and have your deepest secrets revealed. This journal is turning out to be no different. I've already had one friend of mine take issue with something I've written, and then yesterday someone thought my review of Friday's show at Schwarzer Hermann was "negative."

Let me set the record straight: the Schwarzer Hermann show was really good! I enjoyed myself, and I think the crowd there did too. It started out quiet, but picked up as the concert went on. I *like* Schwarzer Hermann!

Also, it seems less and less people are reading/responding to these entries now. That doesn't bother me much. I can't expect people to take the time to read these daily tomes I'm creating. There is one thing to be said for being long winded, and that's that only the committed readers get to know what's really going on. In the long wind can be many hidden gems that the casual skim readers will miss. Anyway, perhaps I will start making these entries shorter. Lord knows I have plenty of other things I could be doing!

I started the day yesterday with a run. The air in the neighborhoods around the artist flat smelled like honey! Yummy! After my run, I was able to get in some rare downtime and watch some Netflix. I watched "Archer." I'm not sure why I watch this show - perhaps because it's so mindless?

Then I drove the tiny car to a town called *"Cruxhaven,"* about an hour away from Bremen. It was a pleasant drive with very little traffic. Cruxhaven is a cute old town.

Georgina, Ripley, Danny, and I all shared the bill at the venue called *"Janja's Musikbar."* It was a fun night! There were about 40 people in the audience. The bartenders were kind, and so was the audience. I really got into my performance, and I even lay down on the floor at the end like I used to do in my 20s! A punk rock star! Good times.

I'll admit, I got a bit carried away with some free alcoholic drinks people bought me at the bar. I was sober by the time I left, but after the show I was hungry. There was nothing open so I went to McDonald's! I never go there! What's happening to me? I justified it to myself by saying, "I have to experience a McDonald's in Germany." It was different. The drive thru menu sign was way different and in German. The people who took my order over the drive thru intercom were cute! It was just a woman at first, then a man's voice came on, and then both of them took my order! Ha! It was funny.

Drove back to Bremen on the Autobahn in the rain, listening to Cut the Cord Radio. I'm enjoying myself.

Day 15: From A Yurt To A Concert Hall

BRIAN LAIDLAW and his girlfriend Ashley are two musicians in the artist flat that I haven't really gotten to know since we all started sharing the flat about 10 days ago. Brian is from the San Francisco Bay area of California, and Ashley is from Minnesota. The two perform Brian's songs together. Brian plays guitar. Ashley plays ukulele. Brian sings, and Ashley harmonizes. The little bit I've heard of them is really pretty, and I like it. Imagine Iron and Wine meets the Moldy Peaches with more of a traveler's edge, and songs about rambling.

Today, I was to share a bill with Brian and Ashley. I showed up to the gig, which was only about a mile away rom the artist flat. It was inside a yurt, within a public square of concrete. Fun! I like yurts, and anything to do with the nomadic lifestyle. The barista at the café, inside the yurt, was friendly. She told me that the yurt was 66 square meters. Her company has two more like it, and an even bigger one (120 square meters) for weddings.

Brian and Ashley set up the equipment. I would be playing first, as I would have to head off immediately afterward to another gig. Since Brian and Ashley would be playing last, they could take their equipment with them. We all sound checked, and had an hour to spare before the show was to start. There was no one in the yurt except for the barista, and us, and about six children who must have lived in the neighborhood because their parents were not around. Brian inquired about their unicycle. I think he tried to ride it, but I'm not sure because I had to use the composting toilet out back, and when I came out there was no more unicycle.

Brian, Ashley, and I had time to finally catch up with each other. After all, we're all musicians from the USA, and we should have plenty of notes to compare. They are planning on moving to Colorado when they return. I told them that I'm not sure if I will be returning to San Diego, or Albuquerque, or Joshua Tree when I get back to the States, as my life seems up in the air at the moment. I'm not sure where will be best for my home base and my music. We had a nice conversation. They are interesting people. Brian is also a published poet, and Ashley does work with community theaters throughout the USA. I hope I didn't come off as a jaded musician to them.

Heiko, the owner of Songs and Whispers, arrived. He's a really cool, tall, German guy who always wears the best boots and pants. I've seen him wear three different pairs of boots out of the four times I've met him now. Boots say a lot about a man. Heiko's say he's a no-nonsense adventurous rebel who likes things done a certain way, and enjoys a good laugh at cultural norms. So far, I'm very impressed with his vision, and how well-run his company is. I can tell a lot of the venue owners on the Songs and Whispers circuit are impressed too. Heiko found out I like cherries and brought me a huge bowl from a cherry tree in his neighborhood! Heiko would be in the audience for the show. I felt a bit of pressure, like, "Gotta impress the record company," kind of thing, but I let it go pretty quickly. At this point in my life, I guess I feel like people can either like my music or not. It doesn't matter to me. I just do my best, and that's all I can do. Besides, there must be a reason Heiko decided to book me for this German tour. He must have a good ear for music. He's a musician himself, having some past success with his electronic metal (?) band.

Once Heiko showed up, the rest of the audience miraculously showed up too. There were probably about 15 people (and the six neighborhood kids) when it was time for me to play. Heiko introduced me in German. All I could understand was "Fast Heart Mart" (which sounds more like "Fahw-st Hot Mot" when Germans say it.) When I started to play my first song, Heiko started messing with my amp settings, adding volume and reverb (I almost never use reverb) and maybe EQ. I was not liking what he was doing, but I gave him the benefit of the doubt, playing my guitar quietly to compensate for too much volume. I did not want to be too loud in this chilled-out yurt/cafe scene. I gave Heiko a few more moments to get things dialed in, but it got unbearable and I had to tell him, "Heiko, that's too loud." He then turned it down and walked away. I've heard from previous artists that Heiko will do this. I think he means well, wanting to ensure that the audience can hear it. Anyway, Heiko walked away, and I got on with the show.

I think the yurt show went well. People laughed at my jokes, and applauded after my songs. People even sang and clapped along sometimes. The audience seemed to have a good time,

Heiko included. I had to tell the neighborhood kids to keep it down once (as they all seemed to be squabbling over the cherries Heiko brought), but they seemed like good kids, and they got quiet when I asked them. Heiko passed the tip jar for me, and I sold some CDs, and it was a pretty fun show. I felt guilty that I had to leave right after I played, and could not stick around to hear Brian and Ashley, but they probably understood.

I then drove to my next gig about 30 minutes away. I played with Georgina and Ripley. It was at a nice theater/concert hall with a tall stage, a nice sounding room, and lights. I was hungry before the concert started, but there was nothing near by to eat. I ate pretzel sticks and beer. I gotta stop drinking beer. Really. It's not my style.

I thought the concert sounded great! The natural reverb of the hall is good! I thought my performance was really energetic and good, as were Georgina's and Ripley's. Georgina and Ripley went on first tonight, which is backwards from how we've been doing it. There were only about 12 people in the audience, and some of them left during my set to go home and watch the football/soccer game. The crowd was pretty nice, but a bit apathetic. It made me think about my overall motto, "People only value what they pay for." Sometimes, people don't value something if you give it to them for free, such as this concert tonight. For example: If I give someone a CD, they may never listen to it. But if I charge them €10, most people will listen to it at least once, maybe even two or three times, before they dismiss it (and by then they might like it.) Same with concerts. If you charge, at least people feel like they'd better get their money's worth. Nonetheless, people did tip, and I think everyone was glad "the show went on." I'm not saying I think we should charge at all of these concerts, I'm just saying, sometimes people get something for free and don't appreciate it.

After the show it was pretty lonely. It's been cold and rainy here today. People were excited about the football/soccer game, and I can't care less about that stuff. I like playing sports, but not necessarily watching them.

I realized today that my cell phone is good for everything except making phone calls! It's good at taking photos/videos, texting, GPS, checking my sites, etc., but it's not good for talking to people because the calls are $0.50/minute. Besides, the time difference between here and the USA is awkward and it's difficult to coordinate a call. I fell asleep while watching "Whatever Works" with Larry David. Seems like a funny movie.

There's a Songs and Whispers meeting tomorrow, and then a day off!

Day 16: Euro Cash

I'VE BEEN PLAYING SHOWS almost everyday and making *some* money on this trip, but how do I deposit it into my bank to pay bills? I spent time today figuring this out. It's a weird thing to have money, and not be able to use it for paying your bills (kind of like being a traveling musician.) Let me explain:

Being a traveling musician is a conundrum. Yes, you meet lots of people, but how many of them do you really get to be close to? How many of them do you *want* to get close to? A traveling musician meets lots of girls, but I'm not interested in casual encounters. I want to be in a monogamous marriage, but what girl wants to be with a man who's traveling all the time? (Unless they travel together! I think that's the only solution.)

The last few days/weeks, I've been having issues with my relationships back home in the USA. Today I've been wondering if all my decisions in Life have been one mistake after another? Should I be further along in my life than this? I've been wondering if the music is worth it. While doing my laundry, the (Hungarian?) neighbor in the apartment below, ran into me. He doesn't speak much English, so we communicated in Spanish, and I don't really speak Spanish. *"Musica!"* I said to him with a smile. He smiled back at first, then got a serious look and said, *"Trabajo,"* ("work," in Spanish.) Yes, music is great, but it's also, work.

What's the purpose of this tour? Make a name for my music? See the world? Explore myself? Make some money? Is this better than a steady nine-to-five type job? I'm pretty sure I can pay this month's bills, but what about next month's bills? Am I ever going to be playing shows to people who know me, know my music, and sing along to my songs like they did when I lived in Albuquerque (to people who want to pay entrance?) Or will I be playing to squabbling neighborhood kids in yurts for the rest of my musical life? Is my biggest challenge in Life the fact that I question everything so much?

I had the day off today and that's always bad for morale on any music tour I've ever done. You think, "A day off! I'll get refreshed, and do something super fun." Maybe some people do, but I always seem to need to rest on a day off which probably leads to too much thinking. At least when I'm playing a concert my music lifts my spirits. I thought I'd get some Netflix time in today, but by the time I was done with all my correspondence (fans, places to sleep while away from Bremen, booking shows, etc.) I only had time to finish watching "Whatever Works" with Larry David. The movie kind of reminded me of myself.

It also rained a lot today. It was nice to see the rain, and was the perfect excuse to chill out, but it still created a somber mood.

Mondays can be tough for musicians. The shows are over. It's time to get into touch with reality, and pay some bills.

I don't want to sound negative. I've had many adventures before: Appalachian Trail; vegetable-oil-powered van across the USA; touring both islands of New Zealand, etc. I know I'm just in a valley right now. *I am fine. I'll be fine.* I'm just being real. What would the peaks mean without the valleys? When an adventure feels like it's in the doldrums, I know it's a good time to sit down, and count my blessings. And that's what I'm doing.

I'm going to enjoy the rest of this tour as much as I can. I've enjoyed it so far. This is the first time I've been to Europe, and I'm really grateful that Songs and Whispers has booked/promoted all these shows for me! It'll be over before I know it.

I *am* living out my dreams! It's not always going to be easy, but it's what I want. Now, let me get back out there and play some music.

Day 17: Here Is The Church, There Is The Steeple. I Showed Up, Now Where's All the People?

"PROBABLY at home watching football/soccer, staying out of the rain, resting up for work tomorrow, on this Tuesday night," God answers with a dry sense of humor.

"Why did you give some of us a talent that seems to be almost impossible to make any money at? Why can't we all be paid just as well as doctors, lawyers, real estate agents, and the guy who invented Facebook?" I ask God. God does not answer this question. So, I ask another question, "Should I play inside or outside tonight, at this venue called *'Stagges'* in *Osterholz-*

Scharmbeck, Germany? The reason I ask is because Brian Laidlaw and Ashley said when they played here last week, they set up outside and they did much better than if they would have stayed inside." Just then, thunder boomed overhead. I decide to stay inside the venue, if for no other reason than I did not want to destroy the amp (that Songs and Whispers provided for me) in a sudden downpour. It was a tough decision until the thunderclap though. There were literally no customers inside the restaurant where I had set up. I could see a few customers milling about outside the window where I stood, but no one was inside. Just as I had found out how to say, "The weather is too bad to play outside," in German, the chef came out of the kitchen and personally brought me my complimentary salad. The chef was from Connecticut originally, but had been living in Germany now for 20 years, waiting for his children to grow up so he could move back to the USA, away from his ex-wife (and the mother of his children), who apparently was from around these parts of Germany.

The loud thunderclap should have been enough of an answer for me, but I asked the chef anyway.

"Hey, do artists usually play outside here, or what?"

"Some do, some don't. You won't want to play outside tonight though, because it's most likely gonna rain," he answered. It felt so good to speak to someone in fluent English! The waitresses at the restaurant were as pleasant and kind as could be, but their English was very limited.

So, I began to play at 7:00 p.m. as my tour rider from Songs and Whispers instructed me to do. There was literally no one in the restaurant except for the waitresses, who would smile sincerely, as I played to an empty room. I would smile back, but it was almost a laughing back at the humor of this situation: I'd traveled half way across the globe to play my music for the wooden floors.

I was happy to play though. I sounded great. I did my most

toned-down style on all my songs, singing an octave down from usual, because even though there was no one there, I wanted to fit into the scene. I was a lounge singer in an abandoned bar in Vegas, and damn it, I was doing my thing. It was great practice. Outside the window, I could see a man sitting on a bench and playing guitar to the people walking by. The people would tip him. As I was about to walk out, with just my guitar and banjo (leaving the amplification behind), to perform acoustically for the few people that were sitting on the patio of the restaurant, it started to rain. It rained pretty heavy. The people on the patio came inside the restaurant and found me playing my music. They had come in time to catch the last 20 minutes of my first set. They were attentive and clapping; all seven of them.

"I'm going to be taking a 15-minute break now," I announced at the end of my first set. I could see the busker was still outside under a tree. I think part of me was determined to not let him go home making more tips than I had. So, I grabbed the closest container I could find for my tip basket, and I headed around the room to collect tips from all seven people. Sure, it felt kind of awkward, but they had listened to my music intently, and I needed to be compensated. Most of them had a good sense of humor about it, except for one guy. This guy said to me, "Why would I tip you? I haven't heard you play yet," in his best English. He had heard me play about five songs, and he even clapped at the end of the songs.

"I stood right there and watched you come and listen to me play," I wanted to tell him, but I didn't want to cause any trouble. "Nice shirt," I told him instead. It was a black shirt that said something about Alcatraz in English. It kind of looked like a prison shirt, except it wasn't orange. I'm not sure what I meant with my comment about his shirt. I did kind of like it, because Alcatraz fascinates me, but I also thought it was pretty tacky. The guy concluded, "I'll tip you when you're done playing." Anyway, the other six people in the "audience" were really cool and interested in what I was doing.

I played my second set in a subdued way, like I had done my first set. It's a good thing I took the tip jar around after the first set, because most people left during my second set, including the guy in the Alcatraz shirt. Alcatraz-shirt-guy never tipped me. New people came in for the second set, and they tipped me afterwards. I handed out business cards, and talked to the people. It felt good.

After the show, I sat down to eat my salad, and talk to a couple of people, when in comes this longhaired, adventure-seeking-looking guy, who asks, "Mart, are you done playing already?"

"Yes, the show was seven to nine p.m.," I answered the guy. I got excited because I thought maybe a fan had shown up to my performance.

"Oh, darn. It's always eight to ten p.m. every time I've been here," said the longhaired man with the long dangly earing in one ear.

It turned out, the man's name was Chris, and he was a writer for a local paper. He was covering my concert for tonight. I was impressed with Chris. He asked if he could interview me and take some photos anyway. I told him he could. His questions were good, because I could tell he'd done some research on me, and had even listened to some of my songs. He knew that I loved Beck's music. The interview turned into more of a conversation, because I had many questions to ask of him as well. He is a local "metal" musician around these parts, and I wanted to get some insights into his outlook on being a musician around here in this day and age. He said that most musicians in this part of Germany have a dream of some day playing in America.

"Did you have to pay money to come here and play? If so, how did you fund it?" Chris asked.

"Sure, I had to pay for my plane ticket here, and I ran a crowd funding campaign to make it all happen. I had to pay a deposit to the booking agency, which I'll get back once the tour is over, and I've fulfilled my obligations to them for booking and promoting the shows. I had to pay for the flat where I'm staying, and I had to rent a car. I paid about $3000 to do this."

"Is it a risk coming here and paying this money? Do you think it's going to even out?" he asked.

"What business can get started without an investment into something? You have to buy equipment, rent a space, hire employees, etc. Why would music be any different?" I asked him in response to his leading me into the proposition that I was sort of paying to play.

"Yes, I think I will break even on this tour, which is good. C'mon man, who's making money on anything anymore? Is Instagram making money yet?" I asked him.

"What do you plan to do after this tour?" Chris asked.

"After the Songs and Whispers circuit, I plan on making my way up to Finland to visit some friends, and perform some shows," I told him. "I don't have any shows booked from July 4th through July 19th, so I might just play on the streets where I can."

"Now that sounds like a risk," Chris said. Chris then tried to help me brainstorm some ides for places I could play and make money on my way to Finland. He was genuinely interested in helping me make it all work out.

"Do you play original music?" I asked him.

"I write original songs, yes, but writing and performing original music is like masturbation: you do it because it feels good to you, but no one else cares, so when you are done you put it on a piece of paper and wad it up and throw it in the trash," he answered. It was a funny answer, but it was also a very depressing outlook on the whole thing.

Don't get me wrong; Chris was a pleasant fellow to talk with. He is very informed about music, music history, and the business. But he seemed defeated, and it seemed like the slant he was trying to get for his story (or himself) was, "See, here are these musicians from all over the world paying to play, yet nonetheless falling on their faces."

"If an American company contacted you and your band, and wanted you to play 30 shows that they had booked and promoted for you in America, but you had to pay for all the expenses, would you do it?" I asked Chris.

He smiled at this question, and then answered, "I'd have to think about that one. I'd probably want to do it, but my band mates and I are getting older. We have marriages and children now, and they'd probably say to me, 'You've got to grow up Chris.' I mean, I'm 35 years old now. You must be in your mid to late 20's?" Chris asked me.

"I'm 39," I answered him with a smile of irony.

We compared notes about other things in the "music business." He walked away giving me the impression that it's a lost cause.

"What about Nick Drake?" I asked him. "He was not appreciated in his time. If he could have lived to be 50 years old he could have seen some financial success," I told Chris as he walked away, wanting to give an example of a musician that everyone loves who could have seen success if they'd just stayed alive, and kept going.

"One year I interviewed a bunch of Songs and Whispers artists and four of them in one year told me their main inspiration was Nick Drake," Chris responded. With that, Chris walked away into the foggy misty night, somewhere in the middle of Germany, in a sleepy ol' German town.

After my show, back at the artist flat, Brian and Ashley were singing harmonies together. It was a bittersweet moment for me. I loved that these two have such a beautiful relationship with each other, and a love for their music, but it makes me wonder if I'm doing something wrong? Why have I messed up all my romantic relationships in one way or another? Why am I still wandering this world alone?

"These questions and many more shall be answered in time," I imagined God quelling me before going to sleep. "For now, be happy you don't have children with someone you're not in love with, or with a certifiably insane woman." This is an allusion to the poor chef at the venue who has lived in Germany against his wishes for 20 years, only to raise two children with an ex-partner.

Tomorrow, I get to have a four-and-a-half-hour drive to a town in Southern Germany called *Darmstadt*, to play at the venue, "Golden Krone" (a brand new venue for the Songs and Whispers circuit.) I like leaving town. I like driving long distances. Songs and Whispers has now provided me with a *TomTom* navigation device, so I don't have to eat through all the data on my cell phone plan.

I plan on listening to Cut the Cord Radio a lot on my drive. I'm not sure why, but it seems like Tyler and the gang at Cut the Cord Radio have not posted a new episode in about three months? Weird? I hope the entertainment "business" hasn't jaded them as well.

Darmstadt, here I come. Please put the football/soccer game away and come out to hear me play. I'll make you laugh. I'll make you cry. I'll make you feel and be happy to be alive, I hope.

Day 18: From Point D To Point T

(A taste of home at Golden Krone)

TODAY, I played a show in *Darmstadt*. As far as I know, the letters "d" and "t" are never next to each other in the English language. For me, it's a complicated combo to pronounce, and it was also a complicated city for me to drive to. Getting from point "a" to "b" is easy compared to getting from point "d" to "t".

I hit the road at 11:00 a.m., figuring I'd have plenty of time to get there and hang out with my accommodation contact named Roland. According to my GPS, it was supposed to take four-and-a-half hours, which would have put me there at about 3:30 or 4:00 p.m. (4:30 at the latest.) Wrong!

Almost as soon as I merged onto the Autobahn, the traffic literally stopped. I sat in the same spot for 15 minutes. Then, there was torrential rain that slowed everyone down because we could hardly see. There were endless roadwork zones that sometimes were so narrow, I thought the semi trucks might just fall on top of me. Sometimes, the roadwork zones had a median of separation from the traffic going the opposite direction that's little more than short plastic walls that would not stop any kind of disaster from happening.

I did my best to enjoy the drive by listening to Cut the Cord Radio. For their 100th episode, they had a musician on there named "Gull." I've never heard of him before, but listening to him play on the show, I became a fan. He's reluctant to describe himself as a one-man band, but he's playing drums, and guitar, and singing all by himself. He's innovative, and creates some amazing soundscapes. The guys on Cut the Cord Radio interviewed Gull, and he was a really chill guy.

Four one-hour episodes of Cut the Cord Radio; a bunch of Spotify listening; 10 traffic jams; three rainstorms; and two Burger King stops later, I arrived in Darmstadt, Germany. It was about 6:30 p.m. I thought my journey to Golden Krone was almost complete, but I was wrong. I had to navigate my way through the city of Darmstadt to find the venue. There were trolley tracks in the road, one-way streets, pedestrian crossings, and bike lanes everywhere! At one point, I took a wrong turn and ended up at a bus/trolley station where cars were forbidden. I tried to retreat from the station as quickly as possible, only to find myself going down a one-way trolley lane, and a trolley was coming my way! I finally just parked my car illegally somewhere, and set out on foot, lugging my huge guitar/banjo case on my back, and my merch/brief case in my hand. I walked for about 20 minutes in a pedestrian mall trying to find Golden Krone. I knew I was close, but I just couldn't find it, exactly. I walked over to a hairstylist smoking a cigarette in front of her beauty salon, and I pointed to the name Golden Krone on my phone. The hairstylist instantly smiled and said in her best English, "Ahh yes, Golden Krone is right there." I looked where she was pointing. Scaffolding for renovation covered the venue. I thanked the hairstylist, "Danke shoen," and scurried to Golden Krone.

Somehow, Golden Krone reminded me of an old Spanish-style bar (a *really* old one, where the bulls might run outside.) The walls were thick concrete/adobe and all the doorways and hallways were narrow. I found the performance area, and introduced myself to the bartender named Phillip. As with just about every bartender I've met in Germany, Phillip was friendly and pleasant. I asked him where I should park my car. He looked perplexed for a minute then answered, "You can pull up outside to load-in, but you'll have to park near the university," he pointed. The university was far. I had already found it when I got lost looking for the venue.

    I went back to find my car. At first I didn't see it where I had left it illegally, and I sort of panicked. But it was just hidden by two more cars that had copied me. Phew! I had everything in my car (passport included), and if that were taken from me, I'd have been in trouble. It's moments like these that I realize how far away from home I actually am.

    I drove around, looking for some legal parking. There were no spaces left in any of the free lots, which were about five blocks from the venue anyway. I looked on the streets, and nothing. I got swept way off course from the venue by the one-way streets and trolley lanes, and ended up under a bridge that I knew was far from the venue, but on the way. Under the bridge I saw an exit that had a parking sign that said, "free."

    "I think that means free in German," I thought to myself, as I made my rash decision to park in this parking lot. I climbed the three flights of stairs to get out of the parking garage, which it turns out, was about three-quarters of a mile away from the venue! I walked all my gear over because I did not feel like driving at all anymore. Besides, I canceled my morning walk today so I could leave early to get here. I got plenty of walking in with this haul from the parking garage.

    I set up my equipment at the venue, and then headed back to my car for another load when a man walking down the street spoke.

"Mart?"

"Yes," I answered. It was Roland. Heiko introduced Roland and me through email. Roland is an old friend of Heiko's who would be letting me stay at his house tonight. Instantly, Roland shook my hand and gave me a hug, and I knew he was a great guy from the first sight of him.

Roland carried some of my equipment from my car for me, and we got acquainted. Roland said he's working on his English. I found it very good. It was rare for us to get stuck on certain words.

Roland invited his friend Yurgen to the show. His friend spoke English too. Yurgen informed me that Golden Krone is a legendary venue in this part of the world, as a lot of great musical acts have performed there over the decades. Golden Krone must be 300 years old, I imagined. When I finally finished setting up my gear, it was 8:45 p.m. I had to go on stage at 9:15 p.m. Roland, his friend Yurgen, and I drank a beer together on the back patio. Roland and Yurgen are some of the kindest men I've ever met. They are about 50 years old, and just as youthful as 18-year-olds (but with professional careers.)

There was a moment on the Golden Krone patio when I had the realization that *I am in Europe now*. I think just the way the patio looked and the way all the people interacted was so foreign to me. I wasn't scared; it was just a realization of some kind. Plus, the beer hit me pretty hard, as I was already exhausted.

I went on stage at exactly 9:15 p.m.! I had no idea what to expect from this crowd. When I was sound checking earlier, there was a group of about 20 people from Spain in front of the stage. The group was loud. I feared that if I played for them, they might ignore me, because they wouldn't be able to hear me. Then they were gone. There were about eight other people scattered throughout the room. I opened up the show mellow with "Desert Dessert." As the song went on, I rocked it harder, to show the few people who were in the room that I was going to enjoy myself on stage whether they listened or not. By the end of the song, there were about 20 people in the room again, and they exploded with applause! Wow! It felt good. The seven-hour drive was now worth it!

"Danke shoen," I said, at the end of the first song. " I am Fast Heart Mart, and I have no idea where the Hell I am, but I think we're close to France, and I'm glad to be here with you tonight," I continued. The crowd loved it, and we all toasted to having a fun night.

"Y'all are a great crowd, I can tell already," I said.

"You say, 'y'all,'" I heard someone say. "She's from North Carolina, and she says 'y'all' too," continued the voice. We all got to talking, and most of the crowd was from Virginia Tech!

"Wow! I'm from Virginia," I told them. The crowd all melted into conversation with each other, and I could feel that everyone was now comfortable. These kids from Virginia Tech were cool. They were respectful and intelligent, and we all had a good time together. They clapped and sang along, and I made good tips and CD sales!

After the show, I met a cool, artistic, and active couple from Darmstadt. They were in the audience, and they seemed to enjoy my music. The woman is a songwriter too. The man told me that he has seen one of my favorite American musicians, Jeffrey Lewis, come through Darmstadt about five times over the years! Finally, I felt like I was connecting to the German underground music scene with this couple! There were a lot of cool people in the audience.

I was exhausted after the show. I walked the three-quarters-of-a-mile to get my car, so I could load up my gear and go back to Roland's house to sleep. I put my card in the slot, to exit the garage, but the gate would not go up! The signs are all in German and the machine for my car blinked something in German at me with exclamation points. "What are you *doing!!*" I imagined the sign was telling me, "Why did you ever park your car so far away under a bridge like this without even knowing if you're allowed to park here?" I was at the end of my rope. I found the nearest parking spot, and slightly scraped my car on the garage walls in haste. Nothing showed up on the car.

I walked the better part of a mile, back to the venue. Roland and the artistic German couple all walked back to the parking garage with me. They showed me the machine to pay for parking. I felt a little stupid, but not much, because all the signs were in German, and even they sort of had a tough time finding the machine to pay.

Roland and I arrived at his place at about 1:15 a.m. I lay down on the couch his wife had prepared for me, exhausted and frazzled, and went straight to sleep.

Day 19: The Hero Bar

(In uniform at Heldenbar with Jim Sallinger)

I AWOKE on Roland's couch this morning at 7:45 a.m. Roland's house is serene and peaceful feeling. Good energy there. Outside, I could hear the hiss of the world toiling - driving in rush hour traffic to get to work on time. Somehow, I imagined I would get to Europe and find that people don't do this toiling. Why would I think that? Somehow, I imagined that I'd get to Germany, and the world would slow down.

I got up, and headed for the bathroom. I was exhausted. I had slept well, but the day before was mentally exhausting. "What am I doing?" I asked myself. As I opened the door, I realized that Roland, his wife, and his 10-year-old son, were sitting in their kitchen eating breakfast together. My sad songs from my album "Farewell Virginia" played on their stereo. I gave myself a pat on the back because I thought I sounded good coming out of their stereo. Hearing myself is a tricky thing. I've produced all my own albums since 2004, and it's hard to get perspective sometimes. Oh man! How precious can this happy little family, listening to my sad love songs at breakfast, possibly be?

"Hello Mart," Roland said, as I almost sneaked by, trying not to disturb them. He introduced me to his wife and son, and he asked if I'd like to join them for breakfast. I declined, as I was not hungry, and was in no mood for socializing in my mental state. Instead, I used the bathroom, and went and lay back down, in hopes of gathering myself to mentally prepare for my drive back to Bremen. I've never imagined that I'd have children, but if I did, I'd want to be like Roland and his family, which means, I'd better go home right now and find a woman and settle down. Roland is 51. He must have been 40 when he had his son. Roland probably did not waste his life gallivanting all over the German Autobahn, playing for perfect strangers. Roland had a vision and went for it, and now look at this beautifully serene house he and his wife have built together.

After about an hour of laying in my emotional cesspool, I gathered myself enough to leave Roland's house, and left a note that said, "Danke shoen," with a smiley, as my token of gratitude for the night's stay. Roland was gone off to work by then. How does Roland do it? He was so energetic the whole night, helping me lug my gear until 1:00 a.m. Then, he got up, had breakfast with his family, and has gone off to drive 300 km to a job he has in Berlin! Roland's wife and son told me goodbye and made sure I got out of their house ok.

I was about a mile from Roland's house when I realized that I was out of gas! I mean the gas gauge did not even have a reading. "There will be a gas station soon," I assured myself, because I had seen plenty on the drive to Roland's house the night before.

The TomTom led me back to Bremen. I reached the Autobahn and still had not found a gas station. I assumed I'd see one off the Autobahn, so on I merged. Five kilometers passed, and still no gas. I resolved to exit at the first sign of *any* business off the Autobahn. I did not want to run out of gas in one of these roadwork zones where there are no shoulders. That would be a disaster! I eventually saw an IKEA, and exited. No gas station in sight, so I yelped one on my iPhone. Fortunately, there was one about one-and-a-half miles away. I didn't need to get back on the Autobahn, but it was a circuitous route there.

After I fueled up, I was ready to hit the open road back to Bremen. Unfortunately, the Autobahn back to Bremen is not really an "open road." Someone explained to me recently that Germany is a relatively small country that is fairly densely populated. That's why a lot of the roads have so much traffic. I've been spoiled by years and years of open roads in the USA, through New Mexico, Arizona, Colorado, Wyoming, Montana, Nevada, Utah, and parts of California. One time, I remember driving through Nevada, and not seeing another car on the highway for an hour. Heaven. However, that's not the Autobahn. Parts of the Autobahn have been open (like from Bremen to Cauxhaven), but from Darmstadt to Bremen, you find traffic, constant speed limit changes, roadwork zones, and semi trucks (I thought Europeans employed trains more for their freight shipping?)

I listened to Cut the Cord Radio on my drive. I'm determined to get through all their existing episodes before I go to Virginia. They've been keeping me great company.

I arrived in Bremen at 2:30 p.m. (not too bad, relatively.) Only five and a half hours today. I was not in the mood for anything. I just wanted to get some sleep. I needed a few groceries, so I picked them up at the crowded grocery store with only two lanes open, and about six people with full carts in each of them. Then I arrived at the flat. No one else was there. I took a shower and a nap, and wrote my journal entry. Amazingly, I somehow felt refreshed and ready for my show at 9:00 p.m. at the *"Heldenbar"* in Bremen.

The Heldenbar is located in a part of Bremen where I hadn't been before. It's an urban area bustling with life and shops of all kinds. There are trolleys running through it, bicycles galore, and pedestrians everywhere. Luckily, I found a place to park close to the venue. Heldenbar means "hero bar," I think. There are pictures of heroes lining the walls of the venue. (Still not sure why Darth Vader was on the wall though?) I found this appropriate because I was feeling like a hero for surviving my trip to Darmstadt and back, and for pulling myself together enough to get to this gig on time.

Last week, Heiko had sent a songwriter my way, via email, named Jim Sallinger (no known relation to J.D. Sallinger. Yes, I asked), from Los Angeles, California. Heiko suggested we share the bill together. I have to admit; I was reluctant about it at first. I'm not sure why. I think songwriters are like cats. You know when you introduce two cats, and they either ignore each other or fight, right away? I feel like songwriters can be like that too. I know I am. I'm not proud of it, but it's how it is. The ignoring and fighting can go on for years/decades. I listened to Jim Sallinger's music online, then wrote and told him it'd be cool to share the bill at the Heldenbar, as long as he didn't expect to get paid (Dang! Sometimes I can't believe I'm operating this way, but the music is my only income right now, and that was my concern. Kind of embarrassing, but true.) Jim wrote back that money wasn't an issue. He just wanted to play a show in Bremen because this is where his wife is from, and they're visiting town right now.

Jim and his wife showed up to the Heldenbar as I was setting up the music equipment. Instantly, I liked Jim and his wife! What a great couple: super chill, respectful, and fun.

Jim played the first set. I really enjoyed his performance.

He's got some fun songs, and he made the few people who were in the audience comfortable. Check out Jim's music here: (www.jimsalinger.com and www.jimsalinger.bandcamp.com)

Tonight was another football/soccer game with Germany playing Poland. There was some sort of Polish fans' parade before the game (with car horns honking ceaselessly), being escorted by the local police force. These football/soccer games are threatening to ruin my entire tour because it seems like everyone here watches the games, and they are slated to keep playing until next month! At one point during the game, while Jim was playing, there was not one person, bicycle or car on the busy street in front of the bar. It was like a post-apocalyptic scene or something. The bartender at the Heldenbar told me it might be a slow night. "Well, hopefully we'll get all the people who don't watch football/soccer," I told him. This bartender was also pleasant, and handsome. I told him he should be a model or an actor. Fortunately, there were a few people who came to the show, who didn't care for football/soccer.

I played my set to the 15 or so people who were there. I told the audience that this was the football/soccer protest concert. I was on my game for sure; telling stories about my European adventure so far. I joked that Jim and I both wore plaid shirts because it's the law in America that songwriters have to wear plaid, so everyone can identify them, and take pity on their poor souls. People clapped along, sang with me, tipped well, and bought CDs after the show. There was a wall with mirrors directly across the room from me, so I got to watch myself perform, and I looked pretty darn good, I must say.

After the show, I spoke to a few locals about my music and such. A doctor named Fredrich introduced himself while buying some of my CDs. He's a dermatologist. He told me that he's a big fan of old American folk music, like Phil Ochs and Buffy Saint-Marie. We talked about how that music may resume again sometime, and that live music will never die. Friedrich then told me that he's written articles about Charles Bukowski! He's a big Charles Bukowski fan, like me! Jim's wife told me that they read Charles Bukowski in high school in Germany! Wow! That's great! We all sat around and talked about German culture. Jim's wife talked about how Germany used to be about 16 different kingdoms, and that's why there are so many different dialects and cultures within Germany. It made me think about how the football/soccer game fills the void for war in some ways because maybe people have to have some kind of war/competition always going on to feel alive. Sport is a step in the right direction towards world peace. We're all being forced to interact with each other now. If we don't destroy the environment, or each other, we may actually be able to achieve world peace!

Then we finished our beers and left the Heldenbar. It was a great night.

Back at the artist flat, as we hadn't seen each other for a few days, Ripley and I caught up - swapping stories about our recent shows and German experiences. Then it was time for sleep, precious sleep.

Day 20: A Good Review From Berlin

(Playing at Bar Unterrock)

DROVE from Bremen to Berlin today. It was a much easier drive than Bremen to Darmstadt, but still a lot of driving. Tired, I arrived in Berlin at about 6:00 p.m. I parked across from the venue, and before I checked in, I laid my driver's seat back and took a nap. Fifteen minutes of sleep can make a world of difference.

I checked into the venue called *"Bar Unterrock."* It's a nice bar in the bottom of an old building, run by accommodating and friendly people. The owner, Harold, showed me around. As he did, Poppy Dames arrived.

Poppy Dames is a singer from Silver City, New Mexico. She moved to Berlin about nine months ago. Poppy and her family used to come see me play in Silver City on many of my New Mexico tours. Silver City feels like a second home to me, because I've played there so many times throughout the years.

I knew I wouldn't have much of a draw in Berlin because I've never played here before. At the last minute, I contacted some other friends and acquaintances that have Berlin connections, but I'm terrible about promoting my concerts, and I should have contacted them sooner. I was relieved when Poppy said she could make it out tonight, and not only that, she also was willing to open for me. Sweet!

Poppy and I finished setting up, and then we had dinner at an Indian Restaurant a few blocks away. I interviewed her about her experiences so far in Berlin. She's courageous to have moved out here straight out of high school at the age of 17. She's only 18 now, and living in a land far away from Silver City, New Mexico. She had friends from New Mexico here already, so she has that going for her.

As Poppy and I walked the streets of Berlin, I could feel the intensity of this city. In Berlin, all the grocery stores close by 8:00 p.m. because the workers unions are so strong. Wow! That's really impressive. I could feel the *un*-apathy in Berlin. I could feel how active this city is about taking care of itself, especially when we walked by a grocery store that was closed at 8:30 p.m. It had been open at 7:30, the first time we passed by.

At the venue, Poppy and I had a beer together. Legal drinking-age here is 16 (18 for hard alcohol.) There was hardly anyone in the bar at 9:15 p.m. The soccer/football game was partly to blame. A man at the bar told me, "Enjoy your life," when I ordered my beer. The man was drunk. A little bit before 9:30 p.m., about 10 of Poppy's friends showed up. I told Poppy to start playing at 9:45.

"Music now? There's no one here yet," the drunken man at the bar yelled at me, then went on to say something else.

"I've been doing this a long time. As soon as the music starts people will trickle in like magic," I retorted. I didn't want to wait any longer. I felt the time was right. I do not like playing way into the night, and I find that serious concertgoers don't either. The really late night is mostly drunken people out on the prowl. I find there's a nice window from 8:00 to 11:00 p.m. for serious music listeners. The man yelled something back at me and I felt like responding, but Harold and the rest of the crew at the bar intercepted the conversation and hushed the man up.

"I'm going to get thrown out of Germany," I said quietly, but out loud to myself. A German woman behind me must have heard me.

"Don't worry, you're fine," she laughed. It was comforting of her to say because I was feeling awkward. The guy who sold me some post cards earlier had given me a bit of attitude, and I was starting to feel like I was stepping on everyone's toes.

Poppy hit the stage. She was fabulous! She sings with the grace of a performer who's been doing it for decades. She has one of those really hushed down tones to her music, and she's not the least bit apologetic or timid about it. Well, she kind of apologized for doing so many sad songs, but we assured her that it was ok, because we all loved sad songs too. She knows what she wants with her songs and she achieves it. I love slow, hushed, sad songs, but I've always felt that I can't do too many of those, or the audience will leave me. The audience stayed with Poppy for her entire performance. I was impressed and delighted to have shared the stage with her.

My set went well too. I started out mellow, careful not to disrupt the mood that Poppy had set so well. People listened. It was a nice concert. I got a bit weird with some of the things I said between songs like, "Hey people, you gotta do what you want with your life because you're gonna die anyway. I'm doing what I want and I'm in Berlin, Germany tonight!" It was pretty good banter, but I felt like some people who don't know me well might have thought I came across as a jaded nihilist. What better town to explore my nihilistic tendencies than Berlin, though?

People clapped, and sang along, and listened attentively.

They tipped well, and I sold some CDs.

After the performance, I was exhausted. I handed out my business cards, and then flopped down on an armchair that was isolated from everyone. I just wanted to go to sleep. I had another beer before I packed up to leave. I talked to Harold and some others at the bar about German history. It's fascinating to hear about all the kingdoms of yore, all the dialects in Germany, and the history of Switzerland in relation to Germany. Good times. Cool people.

Poppy went to work after the show! She gave me her address at the apartment she shares with four roommates. I drove the 15 minutes there. Some of her roommates had been at the show, and some had not. They were all welcoming and accommodating when I arrived to sleep in their living room for the night. I lay down in my sleeping bag on the living room floor because the couches were too short. Sleep came instantly.

(Poppy Dames)

Day 21: A Day Off

I AWOKE on the living room floor of Poppy's apartment, in Berlin, at about 6:30 a.m. I'm not sure why my body insists on waking up so early every morning with the sun (even though I didn't go to sleep until 1:00 a.m.) I wake up with the sun everyday, no matter what. That's why I try to always be in bed by 11:00 p.m. I'm a terrible rock star. I don't like staying up late. I want to be in a monogamous relationship. I reluctantly drink alcohol. I don't even drink coffee to wake me up in the morning. I'm a walking contradiction.

As I had the day off from performing, I kind of wanted to see some sights in Berlin, but I was exhausted. Besides, I did not know what I wanted to see. Did I want to see the Berlin Wall? Not really. A museum? Not really. I wanted to meet other artists and see their studios. I wanted to see where the artists squat and live for free (but maybe I had invented that in my mind? Maybe that happened here a long time ago?) I'm cynical that any place is truly cool if the general public knows about it. Seattle must have been pretty cool before everyone found out about the Grunge Scene. Santa Fe must have been pretty cool in the 70's when scientists from Los Alamos would mingle at the bars with artists. Paris, France was probably cool when all those great painters, and musicians, and writers were alive. New York City must have been cool when punk rock was just getting going. There are great scenes going on all over the world right now, but the general public does not know about them. That's *why* they are cool. As soon as tourists start flocking, it's over, in my opinion. Sight seeing is ok when you've got time, but I'm on a mission of spreading The Word of Fast Heart Mart.

But what of the bear that seems to be a mascot in Berlin? I was told that there are no bears in Germany. Sadly, I think bears have been eradicated from Germany. I think bears used to live in Germany, before it became so densely populated by musicians speeding on the Autobahn. Maybe the Berlin Bear is a reminder of what was (and is yet to be, again?) Either way, it makes me grateful that we have bears in the USA!

I got up off the floor and headed to my car with my sleeping bag, my laptop computer, and all my gear.

My iPhone would not take a charge. I stopped and bought a new cable for €28, but it didn't work, which was annoying because €28 is a significant chunk of what I had made for playing in Berlin the night before. I sort of panicked! What if I couldn't charge my iPhone anymore? I'd be screwed! No more photos, text messages, podcasts, Spotify, Instagram, checking my email and Facebook 13 times a day! I'm reluctant to admit it, but my iPhone is probably my 3rd best travel companion, right after my tiny rental car and my sleeping bag. Without those top three things, I'm toast. I powered my phone off, then back on again, and it took a charge! Phew. I still think something's wrong with the cable jack though. I'd better get that fixed ASAP. I could do without the iPhone, especially since I now have the TomTom to navigate, but it'd be a lot less fun.

I headed back to Bremen on the Autobahn, completely uninspired. I was exhausted and sleepy. I had no more Cut the Cord Radio episodes to listen to because I had listened to the last one on my way into Berlin. It was episode 108 that has no proper outro, just silence (because Tyler and James and everyone think it's bombing so badly.) It's the episode with the description of "Hmmm... this one is umm... well, bad. It is not really funny at all. We are sorry and will try to do better in the future... maybe? Have fun listening to it though!" Ha! These guys are great! Even when they think they aren't funny, they really are. True art, in my opinion, because they're doing it their own way the best they can. They are cool like Howard Stern before he got his book deal (Howard Stern is still great, but it's not the same now.) Like Grunge before The Stone Temple Pilots and Bush took over the airwaves. I'm not sure what's going on with Cut the Cord Radio because they haven't posted an episode since March 27th of this year. That was about three months ago. I hope everything is ok. I'm going to write them and check in.

But today I didn't have Cut the Cord Radio to listen to. I did not want to listen to any music. I was lonely and sleepy. I pulled over at a rest stop after about two hours of driving, bushwhacked my way to a clearing in some trees with my sleeping bag, and took a nap. It helped, but I still felt uninspired.

"The world is overpopulated. Why bother getting married? It could lead to more babies, and there are already too many people. There are immigration/refugee problems everywhere (not an opinion or a stance, just an observation.) The environment is suffering, and I'm part of the problem: driving around in a car; drinking sparkling water out of plastic bottles; eating meat at fast food restaurants; singing songs about whatever I want." All these thoughts clouded my mind as I drove. "I should just find a cave somewhere and live there the rest of my days," I concluded. That's when I checked my email and saw a message from someone who wrote, "Hey, I saw your show last night in Berlin and loved it! Keep doin' what you do, Mart. You can liven any place up, I bet. Rock on! – Berlin." It was enough to lift my spirits. It was a sign from the Universe that I'm on the right track. Besides, I'd get bored living in a cave. I need to be a part of the world, somehow.

After another rest stop, and another nap (in my sleeping bag, in the woods, with the sound of the Autobahn whirring by), I made it back to the artist flat. Ripley and I swapped stories of our travels for the past few days. It was good to see him and Georgina. They were on their way to a gig. I had the apartment to myself for the entire evening. It was perfect. I napped; showered; did my laundry; caught up on some correspondence; had a nice meal; and watched the first episode of "Orange is the New Black: Season Four" on Netflix. It was a good night off because now I'm ready to get back out there and play some music!

It's Father's Day on Sunday. The older I get, the more I look like my dad, which is a good thing, because he's a good looking and hardy dude.

Happy Father's Day Dad! Thanks for everything.

Day 22: Gummy Bears Galore

PLAYED A SHOW at a venue in *Achim* called *"Katakomben."* All three of the musical acts from this tour performed: Georgina Ward and her guitarist Ripley Smith (AUS); Brian Laidlaw with Ashley (USA); and Fast Heart Mart (USA). It was a good show. People in the audience listened, smiled, clapped, sang along, tipped, and bought CDs.

The venue gave us gummy bears. There are so many gummy bears in Germany because a company called *Haribo* invented them here. I love gummy bears and gummy colas (I know they are not vegan because they're made with gelatin), but I can't help but feel guilty that there are no bears roaming in Germany. I'm not judging. I understand how these things happen, but I can't help but feel like I'm part of the problems in the world, and that this tour I'm doing is not helping the world in any way. I know I am helping the world by doing what I'm passionate about, but it's hard to remember sometimes, and maybe I'd help the world more by being an organic farmer, and preserving the bears. I'm fine, but I don't feel like writing anymore today. Uninspired.

Day 23: Migrant Musician?

(Live on the air)

I PLAYED a radio show and a concert today in a town called *Oldenburg*, a university town with a population of about 160,000. The people at the radio station were friendly and inviting. I always feel famous when I do radio and TV appearances. I was on the radio to promote my show that evening. The DJ interviewed me and I played, "I'm An Alien and I Want to Go Home" live in their studio. The station also played a few more of my recorded songs from my albums.

I had a lot of time between the radio show and the concert. Since I'd listened to all the Cut the Cord Radio episodes already, I listened to Marc Maron's podcast "WTF" in my car as I drove around Oldenburg in the rain. I had never listened to this podcast before, but I'm a fan of Marc Maron's. I instantly really liked this podcast. Marc Maron interviews a lot of different people, but mostly comedians. It's great to hear the ups and downs of being a performer, and how comedians make a life out of performing their stand up comedy. Comedians have good nights and bad nights, just like musicians. I could be wrong, but I think more comedians are making a living at this than musicians now? What I mean is, I think single comedians can tour around and make more money than single musicians.

I think the public needs laughter these days. The world is in such a mess at the moment that I think people really just want to laugh. I try to always put some humor into my songs, and I definitely try to get the crowd laughing/smiling with my stage banter. Perhaps I need to take my songs into an even funnier place? I've wanted to try stand-up comedy for a while now. Maybe I could combine my music with stand up somehow?

Anyway, I sat in my car listening to Marc Maron's podcast. I was disenchanted with being on tour. I've lost perspective somehow. I was hungry, as I didn't have time to eat a proper breakfast. I woke up late because I was not in the mood for another day of hustling and bustling. So, I found a McDonald's and ate some Chicken McNuggets while sitting in my car, listening to Marc Maron talk to Chelsea Handler as the rain came down. I've succumbed to eating fast food now, unless I have an interpreter, because I've had some experiences lately trying other restaurants where I've ended up ordering things I don't like. There were homeless people looking at me. I was lonely and disenchanted.

Sometimes, I wonder if I have some kind of entitlement issues? Somewhere inside of me, nothing is ever good enough. I've had some good jobs that I've left because I'm disenchanted. I had a good following for my music in Albuquerque before I left and moved to Virginia. I've had some really good romantic relationships that I've let go of for one reason or another. I live in San Diego, CA, where the weather is the best of anywhere in the continental USA. My parents are just about the best parents a guy could have. I am in good health. I'm a talented musician with good skills and the ability to entertain an audience, so why the disenchantment?

If the world suddenly became a Garden of Eden overnight, and all the extinct animals came back, and we all lived in peace together, and we could pick fruit from the trees, and live a life of absolute leisure, would I still find the problem, and choose to be unhappy? Am I wrong to think that our world doesn't deserve to live like this (no time to spend doing what we really want with the people we want), because we gotta make money? It's a question I pondered before heading to the venue for my concert.

I played at *Litfaß* in Oldenburg. As soon as the owner let me in the front door, I knew it was going to be a pleasant night. The owner of Litfaß is as accommodating and friendly as a person could ever be. He's a German man who speaks English well. He really seemed to care about my well being. It felt good. The owner who takes pride in their restaurant is a beautiful thing to see, and a good role model for those all over the world in these times of upheaval.

I did my sound check, then went to the bar to have a drink that the owner told me about called "Lynchburg Lemonade" (a lemonade drink with Jack Daniel's whiskey in it, and a few other ingredients.) It was really good, even on this cold rainy afternoon. The woman at the bar was kind to me as well, speaking English as best she could to accommodate my non-German-speaking self. I also ate a hamburger because all the reviews of Litfaß's hamburgers were so good. Georgina even called it the best hamburger she's ever had. I haven't had any beef since I arrived in Germany, so I'm not going to feel too guilty. It was a good hamburger.

The owner and I talked about musicians that had played there previously. He told me that a lot of the musicians came from California. Why do so many musicians come form California to play here in Germany and Europe? Are we some kind of migrant musicians who have to travel, because there's not enough work in our own country? It's a profound question! Is our emotional quality of life so bad that we have to seek foreign lands for respite? Do we have something to offer the European audiences that they want/need?

I took a good nap in my car after the Lynchburg Lemonade, and the hamburger, and a good conversation with the owner.

After the nap, I headed inside for the stage. There was a bunch of people in there. When I sound checked, there had been no one. Now, there must have been 30 people around the stage, plus another 20 at the bar, and 15 in a side room. Dang! I was wearing my glasses because I forgot to get some contact lens solution.

With all the mysterious confidence that I had, I did not introduce myself before I played my first song "Desert Dessert." The people around the stage were eating and talking quite a bit and I felt like I was too quiet, so I turned up. My first set went ok, but I felt like people were more into their food and their company than my music. I knew within the first three songs not to waste my energy competing for their attention. Sometimes you just gotta let people enjoy their meals and company. This isn't a concert after all; this is a restaurant with a stage.

Earlier, during sound check, I had decided not to use Litfaß's PA system. I didn't know what kind of shape it was in, and I didn't see any monitors, so I figured it was defunct. If I could do it over again, I would use Litfaß's PA because my amp wasn't quite loud enough.

My second set went better because people were mostly done eating and talking, and now they were ready to listen to me. I said some fun stage banter including, "Moine, moine," and I got people clapping and singing along, and the room came to life.

I made some decent tips, and sold quite a few CDs. It was a good show, especially for a rainy Monday night with soccer/football showing in the next room over. Afterward, I met a cool guy named Neil who says he was named after Neil Young.

A woman in the audience mentioned Jeffrey Lewis again

tonight. Apparently, Jeffrey Lewis has been getting around Germany and is becoming pretty well known here. Good for him! I like Jeffrey Lewis a lot.

I'm just going through the motions right now. I have faith I'll be re-inspired soon. I look forward to the day that I can show up for a concert and the majority of the crowd knows my music, and me, already.

Day 24: On The Upswing At A Church Concert

(Rockin' the church crowd)

YES, THAT'S RIGHT! I'm back in the groove with this tour. I had a fabulous night playing at a church in a town called *Rotenburg*. There were about 40 people there in the pews, listening attentively, singing along, and clapping to the beat. You could have heard a pin drop at times. You could feel the joy in the air. My cowboy hat was filled with money at the end. I needed this night. Danke shoen!

After a few days of constant ups and downs, today was a

great and strong day. I went for my morning run and even that was stronger than it's been for the last week.

I arrived at the church in Rotenburg, at about 5:45 p.m. There was a man there named Frank, who showed me around the church. I set up my equipment in the beautiful, huge, congregation hall. I knew this show was going to be special, so I set up three video cameras that I hope to edit into a video to show the world.

After I set up, Frank and I had a beer. I've succumbed to the fact that having a beer is a great way to interact with people in the world, even if it is at a church. Frank's English is pretty good, but I get the feeling he doesn't get the opportunity to use English often. Frank and I discussed the bear situation in Germany. Frank, too, is displeased that bears no longer wander the German countryside. However, he assured me that wolves still roam. Yay! The beer we drank must have donated some of its proceeds to a wildlife foundation because there were pictures of critters on the labels.

As I wrote before, the show went great. I could see that the 40 people who showed up had a great time. The crowd lifted my spirits and I lifted theirs. A symbiotic relationship!

I did not mention, to this obviously Christian audience, that I am a Baha'i. I felt it unnecessary. The Baha'i faith teaches all religions should focus on their similarities, not their differences. I did talk about other religions in a respectful way to allude to the fact that I don't believe that Christianity is the *only* way. I introduced "I Am a Sky Blue Flower," with a story about its writer, a spiritual master from India named Sri Chinmoy. It was a beautiful moment when we all sang "Sky Blue Flower," together.

I'm starting to feel a bit like Pete Seeger, which isn't necessarily a bad thing, though I've never drawn much inspiration from him before. Pete Seeger was great at getting a crowd of people to clap and sing along at his concerts, and people had a great time. I never imagined myself to be this type of performer. Whatever. I'm gonna go with it. It makes me happy to see people enjoying themselves in such a wholesome way.

I can hear people criticizing me for playing in a church to mostly older people. "You what?" I saw The Old Crow Medicine Show in 2005 (before all the hipsters in the tattoo shops even knew who they were), and they were playing for similar audiences back then. Older people know what's up, are willing to take a chance on hearing something new, and have the money to support it, so there. (WARNING: Tangent below. May be boring to you. Not necessary to read to keep up with the journey.)

I've mentioned this before, but writing this journal/diary for the world to read has been tricky business. I want the world to know how I feel, but also this journal is an exploration of myself. If I write that I'm not sure where I'm moving to next it does not mean that I'm not going to return to San Diego. Some people go on vacations and share images of themselves smiling at the Eiffel Tower, London Bridge, Grand Canyon, etc. But I wanted my journey here to show that travelers also think about leaping from the tops of those tourist destinations because Life can be painful, even when you're on vacation. I'm joking about leaping from the Eiffel Tower, but you know what I mean.

So much of social media is fluffy highlight reels with no sign of tension or turmoil, like a walk through Disney World (I've actually never been to Disney World or Disneyland because I've never had the desire, even when my parents offered to take me as a child.) No wonder social media can be so depressing for some of us whose lives are not plateaus of happiness and serenity.

I think it is my duty as an artist to show the world that it's ok to be a human being. Humans make mistakes. We feel ways that we don't want to. We ask questions about things we don't understand. We are happy sometimes and sad at other times. It's the tension and release of Life that makes things interesting.

It has been said that good music is essentially tension and release. What would that chorus mean without the verse? How interesting would the song be without a minor chord thrown in at just the right moment to help us celebrate the victory over the pain? And so is Life. We must dwell in the light, but acknowledge the darkness if it's going to be at all fulfilling.

This is why I've chosen to write these journal entries as honestly as I can. The last thing the world needs is another musician telling the world how absolutely great his trip to Europe was, just to boost his status so all the people in the USA take him more seriously and say, "He's a big deal in Europe." We need to see the struggle. We need to see that some of the shows had very few people in the audience. We need to see the triumph over self-doubt on a daily basis. We need the world to see the truth of being a human being. We need the world to know that there are more actors than Brad Pitt and Johnny Depp who can play those roles. There are many artists on this planet and they all deserve a place. It is our duty as artists to be radically honest now, and face the consequences that may come from that. Consequences make for the tension and release, and within that tension and release exists the consequential *beauty*.

Perhaps it is my fatal flaw that I don't enjoy hiding my cards from the other poker players? You want to see my cards? Here! Look at them. I welcome your help for my next move so I can win. I don't really like poker. It's a game of posturing to see who can hide their body language the best using a hand of cards dealt randomly. Our relationships with each other are conducted so often like a poker game, especially romantic relationships. Hide those cards until someone gets trumped and guns start blazing in haste. I'm a chess player. Pure skill wins that game.

I'm glad you are all reading this. I'm honored, grateful, and flattered. Take some of my questions and doubts with a grain of sand (I've never understood the "grain of salt" saying, but there are many grains of sand that drip through the hour glass.) I'm not clinically depressed. This has been an adventurous trip with lots of unpredictable delights and I'm glad to be on it.

Day 25: The Most Intimate Concert Yet

(Getting intimate at Zum Fas)

TONIGHT, I played a show for three people at a corner bar on a fabulous summer night in Bremen, Germany. I think the soccer game and beautiful weather kept everyone at home. Last night's show at the church in Rotenburg was so lucrative, it was ok that tonight was slower. Even though there were only three people who sat and listened to me tonight, I felt good. I'm doing my thing. I'm honoring my gift. I'm practicing. I'm honing my craft. The three people listened attentively, and clapped and sang along. I made pretty good tip money because the man who was in charge of the show named Heiko (a different Heiko than the one from Songs and Whispers) took the tip hat around to everyone inside the bar, even though they could not hear me outside. Heiko is a pleasant man. I love his enthusiasm, and he spoke his best English to accommodate me. He even told me that one of my songs reminded him of Nirvana, which I really liked to hear.

Getting paid with tips night after night is all fine and good, but sometimes I do feel like a beggar when the people tipping me are in another room where they can't hear me. I guess I should just believe they are tipping me for my cause of lugging myself half way around the world to play music.

I also felt like a beggar today when I went into downtown Bremen to find a bank to turn my coins into bills. I have consolidated about 20 pounds of coins into a paper bag that I carried all over downtime Bremen. The first bank cashier I went to was nice about it, saying, "We do not turn your coins into bills unless you have an account here, but you could try some other banks in the city center." I went to about seven banks within the city center. When I'd walk in, I'd say, "Hallo, speakansie English?" Most of the bank tellers would answer with a smile and say, "A little." Then they'd politely say, "We don't do that without an account, sorry," as if these coins were not money. One woman was super rude when I asked, "Hallo, speakansie English?"

"Dutch ist beta," she answered, or something like that. She looked at my bag of coins and abruptly said, "No, we don't do that here." What the heck? So rude! Keep on believing in the banking system, lady. It's gonna be great when it all comes tumbling down and you have to start being kind to people to survive, instead of upholding some stupid rules at a bank that does not care about you at all. Sorry. It's frustrating to experience so many people believing in a system that only benefits the super rich. The slaves are enslaving each other now, and the slave owners don't have to do anything but sit back and watch it all take place.

Alas, I was not able to cash in my coins anywhere.

While I was downtown, I had to look for a cable for my external hard drive. I ended up at a mall down there, and it was a scary place too. All malls freak me out (too much commercialism all in one place.) I look around in malls and see workers in there under fluorescent lights, and surrounded by merchandise, selling products for the rich owners of the business, and I ask myself, "Do these people really want to work here? Can they really be fulfilled and happy here?" It makes me want to run every time.

I did see/hear a busker down there who sounded good. He had a powerful and clear voice that impressed me. He sounded like he may be from Ireland. He was dressed like he had been sleeping on the streets, as he rambled though Europe. I wasn't in the mood to cross to his side of the street to throw in a tip, but now I wish I had.

Yes, downtown Bremen was a surprisingly overwhelming experience for me. I figured, coming from the USA, that a small downtown city center like Bremen would be fairly tame. Nope. I was completely disoriented within five minutes of being surrounded by tall buildings, trolley lanes, bike paths, and pedestrian crossings. I had to pay to park my car on the 11th floor of a parking garage. I couldn't read how to work the machine to pay for parking, so I asked some teenagers for help.

When I was trying to navigate my way around in my car in downtown Bremen, a man behind me in a Mercedes was beeping his horn, throwing up his hands at me in my rear view mirror. We came to a red light, and he pulled up to the left of me. I rolled my window down and glared at him with a look of, "Don't even try anything man, I wasn't going that slow. This isn't the Autobahn." The man looked over at me and yelled something at me in German.

"Ha ha ha!" I laughed. "Yell and scream all you want dude! I can't understand a word of it," I yelled back at him with a look of complete confidence that he was wrong for trying to bully me with his Mercedes Benz. Neither one of us said anything more. It was ridiculous.

I finally made it back to the artist flat and chilled out. It's experiences like these that make me concerned more and more for the world. What are we doing? Why do we agree to live like this? Why do we keep having children if we're going to subject them to all of this?

Anyway, the show at *"Zum Fas"* was great tonight. I sat and had a beer with a local musician, named Reiner, after the show. He's currently recording an album of German folk songs that sounds interesting to me. The bartender/owner had a nice smile when he served me beers.

Germany in June is a pleasant place to be on a night like tonight, at the corner bar called Zum Fas.

Day 26: Backstage Divo!

ALL MY SHOWS have been very close to the artist flat in Bremen, Germany this week. I'm glad, because I don't have to spend so much of my time driving. I've enjoyed some much-needed downtime this week.

Today, I took a five-mile walk to the Songs and Whispers headquarters. It was a beautiful summer day here with green trees and grass, warm sunshine, and birds singing. I felt really good.

I played a concert at a community art theatre about 15 minutes away from the artist flat tonight. A man named Henrik showed me around the facility, and he was really pleasant. He's a drummer in a rock band (and he privately plays ukulele.) After I did my sound check and stage lighting, Henrik showed me to the backstage area.

I love having a backstage area! I get my own bathroom, and a place to gather my thoughts in private before I play my concert. I don't care if everyone thinks I'm a divo, I really cherish having a backstage area. I hung out and caught up on some writing and correspondence, then Henrik brought me dinner, and then it was time for my show.

It was another extremely intimate concert tonight, with seven people in a small movie theatre that was way too hot. Football/soccer and good weather (the usual culprits) had caused the low attendance. I played one long one-hour-and-fifteen-minute set, instead of the usual (two 45-minute sets.) It was a good time. People listened, and clapped and sang along, and tipped enough money, and bought seven CDs. Seven CDs is a lot of CDs considering there were only seven people in attendance. Yay me! I'm making German fans one intimate show at a time.

One guy I spoke to after the show is a banjo player. He says he listened to my music on Spotify and then came to the show tonight! Feeling good.

Day 27: Two Encores Tonight!

I HAD TWO ENCORES at the end of the show tonight in *Duisburg*, Germany at a venue called *"Grammatikoff!"* It was a great night! There were about 25 to 30 people there, and they really enjoyed my music. They sang along, clapped along, smiled, tipped well, and bought CDs.

My friend Angela came to the show. She was in London for her job, and it was her birthday. It was nice that she came and saw one of my German shows.

There seemed to be a lot of bad news going on in the world today. One of my all time favorite banjo players and singers, Dr. Ralph Stanley, died. The UK decided to leave the European Union. Their prime minister resigned and their currency plummeted in value. It feels like it's a strange time to be in Europe right now with this news from England, and the Syrian refugees, and there was a mass shooting in Frankfurt, Germany, this week.

Musically, things are going very well. I don't want the tour to end!

Day 28: They Provide the Audience, I Provide the Show

IT WAS ANOTHER GREAT NIGHT of music in Germany! Tonight I was in a town called *Brake*, at a little bar called *"Harrier Hof."* I thought the show was going to be a complete bust because the owner told me there was a big concert of German music (called *Schlagger*?) going on nearby. The owner also said the rain was going to deter people from coming out. I've been having a lot of good shows this week, and I've made good money, so I nonchalantly told the owner, "Shit happens," to let him know that I wasn't going to throw a fit if no one showed up. The owner laughed immediately. I found out a few weeks ago that just about every German knows the phrase "shit happens," even if they don't speak much English. Ha ha!

Up until about 20 minutes before my concert began, there were only two people and the waitress at the venue. I prepared myself for a slow night, sitting outside in my car behind the bar drinking a beer in the rain.

Suddenly, about 15 minutes before the concert started, all these people came in! I started the show right on time, and people were still coming in. The place was pretty much full about three songs in to my concert! There were probably 30 people in the smallish room listening intently. Wow! It was another great audience that clapped along, sang along, smiled, tipped well, and bought my CDs. They called for two encores again at the end of my 45-minute set! I'm feeling really good about my skills as a musician right now. Give me an audience and I'll provide the show. The audience leaves the show feeling uplifted, and so do I. It's a very nice symbiotic relationship.

I met some cool people tonight. A guy named Lars, who I met at the *Hamme Forum* concert two nights ago, came out to hear me again!

Tonight, there was a German guy in the audience who spoke English really well. He heckled me a bit throughout the show, in a good-natured way. I could tell he was into my music, and that he wanted to engage more. We talked awhile after the show. He told me something I found interesting. He said that Germany sold a lot of the weapons to Syria that have caused all the Syrian people to become refugees and that's why he believes that it's Germany's responsibility to take care of them.

"There are one million Syrian refugees to 80 million Germans," he said. "I think 50 Germans can take care of one Syrian refugee," he continued. I'm paraphrasing what he said. He was a very intelligent guy.

This tour has not been easy, but it's really inspiring me to get back out into the world with my music. I had to drive almost five hours in the rain on the Autobahn to get to this show tonight. I had to drive a little over four hours to get to the show the previous night. By the time I'm done driving, I've forgotten what I've come for a lot of the time. But as soon as the show starts, and the music gets going, it all makes sense. Besides, I really like all the time driving. It allows me to listen to music and podcasts.

As many of you know, I've been crusading for a while for "Gentle Yet Dignified" music concerts. I think there are a lot of people in the world that would like to go hear independent/obscure artists, but they don't want to be subjected to the many uncertainties that can come with that experience: too loud; too late; sports screens blaring throughout a crowded bar that's not respecting the music; drunken brawls occurring; too expensive, etc. I think the Songs and Whispers circuit is in line with the concert series I started in San Diego.

There are only four more shows left on this Songs and Whispers tour. I wish I could keep on doing this. I can't stand booking and promoting shows, so it's really nice to have Songs and Whispers do this for me. They provide the audience and I provide the show, and I like it a lot.

Songs and Whispers has created a brand here in Germany that attracts a crowd of people to each of the shows. I think people feel like, "If this artist is on the Songs and Whispers circuit they must be pretty good, and I'm gonna go check them out." It's great! I think the number one criticism people have about Songs and Whispers is that the artists have to pay their own way. Guess what people? Almost every musician has to pay their own way now. Didn't Justin Beiber's mom have to pay for a plane ticket to get Justin Beiber in front of Usher? Isn't crowdfunding the norm for most musicians to make an album these days? Which band doesn't have to buy/rent a tour van? Aren't record companies a type of moneylender that lends money to musicians that must be paid back with interest? Either way, I feel like this trip may actually pay for itself, and then some. As far as I've known, for a long time, most musicians can only hope to break even on tours until they get their "big break."

The old music business models are gone. New ones are being built. I think Songs and Whispers could be creating a new model. Songs and Whispers may even be an old model that is being revived from before recorded music existed? Ever heard of the old "Chitlin' Circuit"?

This tour has inspired me to give it my best shot to play music full time when I return to the USA. It'll be tricky without a booking and promotion company behind me, especially in the USA where audiences are way different than they are here in Germany. But with enough perseverance, I can make it happen. My friend Justin Werner makes his living playing music around San Diego, so I know it is possible. It doesn't look easy, but I know it is possible. My friend Nathan Payne is now touring around full time with his music. I know it's not easy, but he's doing it! The Handsome Family has made a life playing their music all over the world.

I'm grateful to all the day jobs I've had over the years. I've had some really good ones. They've all taught me a ton, and helped me answer some questions about myself. I know what it means to be a "workin' man" as I've certainly paid my dues in that world. Day jobs have allowed me to survive while I learn more about the world, and myself. I'm proud to have helped certain companies in their endeavors. Now it's time for me to finish building my own business.

I would like to continue my audio and video production services as a supplement to my income, but only projects that have a definite beginning and an end. I imagine I will still take some "odd jobs" here and there, but only tasks that have a definite beginning and an end. Then I would like my artistic endeavors to completely phase out my need for "odd jobs" and "day jobs." Perhaps the absence of an end is what troubles me most about the "day jobs"? Perhaps more people would feel more fulfilled by jobs that had a definite beginning and an end?

Q: Why do I want to be a musician/artist full time?

A: Because I'm exhausted from dividing my attention between a day job and my music. I've tried letting go of my music/writing/artist side and working a "real job," but my soul will not let me. Being an artist is the most important thing for me and it's time I let it happen completely. It's time for me to allow myself to focus all my attention on being an artist. I believe it's the only way I'll ever truly feel fulfilled in this world where we are forced to work our lives away in the name of earning money. If I have to work my life away, then I want to do it as an artist. My bank account and my wallet are as full of money as ever, so I'm gonna keep on trucking' down this road and see where it goes.

Day 29: The Grand Finale Concert!

SORRY MY PHOTOS have been kind of lo-fi lately. I'm doing my best to document the performances in the low light situations.

Tonight was the Grand Finale of the Songs and Whispers Tour. All the artists from this tour had a show together at "Club Moments" in Bremen, Germany. It was a lot of fun! There was a pretty good amount of people in the audience.

Brian Laidlaw and Ashley started off the show. The crowd was so attentive you could have heard a pin drop while they were performing, which is a good thing because Brian's excellently lyrical folk songs, with Ashley harmony vocals, deserve people's undivided attention.

Georgina Ward and Ripley Smith were second in the line up. They rocked the crowd with Georgina's upbeat songs and captured the audience's attention with her slower melodic songs such as "Sun and the Moon." Everyone loves Georgina Ward and

Ripley Smith!

I talked to the lighting girl before my set and arranged for her to shut off the lights when I started my set. I turned my back to the audience as Heiko introduced me. Then, the lights went off. There was complete blackness, except for my "Fast Heart Mart" merch case sign. With the lights out, I put on my sunglasses and gently started my guitar riff for my song "Desert Dessert." As the lights slowly faded on, I played my guitar riff a bit louder and suddenly the audience could see me on the stage, standing near the microphone stand, sunglasses on. I started singing the opening line to the song, *"A cactus/ flower/ is blooming/ on the side of the road /we drive /through this/ deserted desert..."* It was a spectacular moment!

My set was a lot of fun. I couldn't tell how many people were in the audience because the lights were too bright, but from what I can gather, there were probably 30 people there, listening intently. The audience clapped along and sang along, and laughed at my jokes, and it was a good time for everyone.

At the end, all the performers came up, and we performed "Stand By Me."

It's not easy to do this tour circuit, so all the performers were proud to have made it to this grand finale with our sanity somewhat still intact.

This is not my final show of the tour though. I still have three more shows on the Songs and Whispers tour circuit this week, and then I'm on to other performances on my own!

After the show, I sold some CDs and made some new fans. When everything was done we all went out and had a drink together. I've had a few beers here and there on this tour, which is uncommon for me, but tonight was even more uncommon. I have to admit, I got a bit drunk, as I was ready to cut loose. I met a man who was cool from the get go. His name is Julian. He wore a great cardigan that looked good on him. He reminds me of a White Barrack Obama. I think he might be the president of the

European Union someday, as he's as personable as a man can be, and he can talk about any subject that comes up. Ripley and Julian, and Julian's friends, all went outside in the street in front of the bar to smoke and speak about rock and roll. It was great to be hanging out with this great group of guys.

Then it was time to go back to the flat. Ashley was the designated driver because we all know better than to even think about drinking and driving.

Julian gave me his green cardigan! I've wanted a cardigan for a while now. Years? Cardigans are like hoodies without the hood. You can wear a cardigan anywhere. Thanks Julian, wherever you might be now.

All the artists hung out in the kitchen of the flat. I ate chili SIN Carne out of the can because I hadn't eaten dinner. We all said goodbye to Georgina and Danny, who are leaving early in the morning, then we all went to sleep at about 2:00 a.m.

Gute Nacht.

Day 30: Where's Your Cowboy Hat?

AWOKE FEELING a bit hung over from the late night, and drinking the night before. I walked five miles to my car, where I had parked it to avoid drinking and driving. I like taking long walks in the morning. It's good for me. As I walked, I thought, "No more drinking like that. That was an exceptional night and now I'm going to get back to the straight and narrow." I was being kind to myself. I could have beaten myself up for getting so drunk. I'm reluctant to drink. Amongst many reasons, alcohol is against my Baha'i beliefs. It's not good for my emotional and physical health, and I think it allows people to avoid real communication, but I gotta let loose and join the crowd sometimes.

    I drove an hour-and-a-half to Hannover to play at a radio show. The formula has sunken in: drive on the Autobahn and listen to a podcast or music until I get in the inner city (where buses, and trolley cars, and bicycles, and pedestrians, and other cars, and one way streets, all make driving a nightmare); find my destination; and (hopefully) a place to park, without having an accident. It's a small miracle every time I arrive to a radio show unscathed, on time, and ready to be interviewed, and to play a song live into a microphone in a room that is inadequate to be capturing my performance. Just play the CD. I love playing, but who knows what it's gonna sound like?

I sat at on a couch with my huge guitar/banjo case at the radio station in Hanover, waiting for someone to tell me what was going on. There were girls speaking German all around me. I wasn't in the mood to ask at first, but then I spoke up.

"Anyone speakanzee English?" I asked, to no one in particular. A girl hesitated to answer, then said, "Yes."

"I'm looking for Andrea," I said, trying to get to the bottom of what was going on.

"I'm her," she answered.

"Ok, I'm Fast Heart Mart. I'm here to play music."

Then a man entered the scene and said, "Oh, you're Fast Heart Mart? I am the DJ for the show that you will be on today. Where is your cowboy hat?"

"It's not stuck to my head," I said. "I figured since this is radio I wouldn't need my hat because there's no sun in here and it's not a cold day".

The DJ then went to another room and came back with a paper king's crown.

"Ok, how about you wear this?" he asked.

"Nope," I told him. I learned a long time ago to never let the entertainment business change you. This was a perfect way for me to put my foot down and show everyone that I had my power too.

The radio show was actually pretty fun. The DJ turned out to be a decent guy with a good sense of humor. He said he felt like "An Alien and I Want to Go Home."

Then I played at a record store 30 minutes after the radio show. Record stores are rare in the USA anymore, even more rare to have one host a Fast Heart Mart in store performance. The people at the record store were very kind and respectful. I played for 30 minutes to a crowd of about 10 people who almost all bought a CD afterwards.

After the record store performance, I headed over to the music venue that I performed in tonight. The venue is called *"KulturPalast"* in Hannover, Germany. The TomTom wanted me to turn the wrong way down a one-way street and I found myself lost once again in some dense city center pedestrian mall with trolley cars, and buses, and bicyclists crowding me. Then the TomTom wanted me to cross a bridge that was closed, so I had to get out my iPhone and pay for the data to guide me to the venue. I finally made it to the venue about five minutes late. Arne, my liaison from Songs and Whispers, called me on the phone to ask if I was ok, just as I reached the venue door. Ha ha. (Perfect timing, Arne.)

When I arrived at the venue, it appeared to be empty. Then I saw a man raise himself up from a napping position on the bench, on the sidewall, and walk over to me.

"Welcome to the club. I'm Michael," said the grey haired man with a beer in his hand at 7:00 p.m. at night in Hannover, Germany. "I'm not sure how many people will be here, since it's raining, and it's Monday, and there is a soccer game on tonight," he continued talking. If only he knew how many times I've heard that in the past four weeks. "But you already have one fan over there," and he pointed at a man who sat at a table alone, drinking a beer.

"Thank you," I answered. Michael seemed kind, but I was not convinced that he knew what was really going on. He helped me get set up and showed me around to the bathroom and the back stage. He was very hospitable. I still wasn't convinced that he understood the magnitude of the situation, namely that I had driven an hour and a half to be here tonight so I could play music. Was he capable of running my sound? Whatever. I was appreciative for his hospitality.

Then I talked to the man who had come to hear me play. He was a man who had heard me on the radio that afternoon. "Let me buy you a beer," he said. We talked over a beer.

The man was named Wolfgang. What a great name! I have never met anyone named Wolfgang before. He said he had heard me on the radio that afternoon, and really liked what he had heard, and wanted to come hear me play the concert tonight. As we shared travel stories, other people came in and we all started talking together. I asked people's names as they came in because I was fascinated by the names. There were two women named *Birtig*, or something similar. I've never heard that name before either.

Michael played the artist known as "Fink" before I went onstage. I like Fink a lot! I think he's brilliant. Michael played a lot of good music and showed me some of his favorite gems that he had acquired through the years.

Completely exhausted and bleary eyed, I played the concert. There were about 20 people at the show (pretty good for a rainy Monday night with football/soccer on TV.) The lights were bright on stage, so I wore my cowboy hat *and* sunglasses. I feel disconnected from the audience when the lights are so bright. I can't see their faces and how they're reacting. I imagine a lot of performers are used to this scenario, but I am not.

I broke a string in the middle of my second song. I tried to banter with the audience while I changed it, but I wasn't in the mood. The audience was quiet as I changed the string. I feared I'd loose their attention. When I finally had the string changed, I sang a song called "Hate Job" that I thought might be good comedy relief. They found it mildly funny.

"Is everyone ok?" I asked. I was wondering why everyone was so quiet. Had I done something wrong that caused everyone to be so quiet? Everyone was fine. They were just really attentive to the music. It's great that audiences are like this here in

Germany. I wish I could get more audiences to be this attentive in the USA.

The show was a success. People clapped, and sang along to the music. They smiled. They laughed. They tipped well. One person in the audience wants to hire me for a house concert in the next week or so, but she told me that I couldn't play "Hate Job" because she thinks people in Germany won't like it. Hmmm. I don't like being censored, but she was a kind lady otherwise, so maybe I should just suck it up and play the house concert?

I hung out after eating a vegan kabob wrap that a very kind man from Turkey had bought me. Michael kept on playing great music on the sound system. I really respect his taste for music. He really gets into music while he's drinking beer and smoking cigarettes! I wasn't sure about him at first, but by the end of the night I realized that he is a passionate music fan who is doing a great job hosting the music at KulturPalast.

I headed back to Bremen at 11:30 p.m. It's an hour and a half drive from Hannover to Bremen. I had to pull over and sleep three times. I'd sleep for 30 minutes, and then drive for 30 minutes. It took me three hours to get to Bremen this way, but I finally arrived to the artist flat at about 2:30 a.m., exhausted.

Day 31: Winding Down

I WOKE UP as early as I could after my three-hour drive from Hannover last night. It was exhausting. I've had that happen before after playing a show in Santa Fe, New Mexico. I thought to myself, "It's only a 90-minute drive, I can do this," only to find myself struggling to stay awake, 30 minutes later.

I showered and headed to Hamburg for a radio interview to promote my show in Hamburg tonight. I battled the typical German inner-city mayhem of sudden one-way streets, trolley cars, pedestrian crossings, and bicycles, everywhere. I even had to back out of a one-way street at one point because it dead-ended at a construction site. I had to make all the cars behind me back out as well. People were pissed! I have no idea why I had to be the first one to come upon the construction site that closed the road. Furthermore, there were trash trucks blocking all the traffic. It's chaos driving in these German inner cities, finding places I have never been before.

I finally found the radio station and parked in a spot that was obviously reserved for someone much more special than me. I could not find a parking space anywhere else, so I wrote a note and left it on my dashboard that read as follows, "I'm not sure if I parked correctly? I am a musician doing a radio show until 3pm June 28 2016. Thank You. www.fastheartmart.com".

I went into the radio station. The DJ told me to wait in the reception area as he was setting up a full rock band to play live on his show today.

"Usually we have a green room for you to wait in, but it is occupied today, so if you'll please just wait at the reception desk I'll come get you when it's time." I waited with Brian Laidlaw and Ashley for about an hour and a half before it was time for me to go on air for the five minutes before the show ended. The DJ played some of my CD and asked some questions.

As I was leaving I asked the band that played before me "What's the name of your band?" They answered, some strange name. "I'm never going to listen to your music because you stole my chance of playing live on the air," I joked with them. They seemed like a nice group of young guys and we laughed at the situation.

Brian Laidlaw and Ashley and I played at a big open-air market in a great part of Hamburg tonight. It was fun! People listened intently and we all sold CDs. A girl after the show gave me a drawing she made of me.

Overall, things are winding down for this leg of my European Tour. I'm on to Cologne tomorrow, for my last show with the Songs and Whispers circuit.

Day 32: Hello, Köln

(The cathedral in Köln looks like a spaceship – Handsome Family)

I SAID GOODBYE to the rest of the flat mates today as I left for Cologne because I do not plan on returning to this part of Germany any time soon. I think I'm gonna miss Ripley the most. I feel like I connected with him so much sharing the tiny room and stuff. He's a great guy and a super talented musician who I have no doubt will make the musician thing work for him.

Then I went and said goodbye to everyone at the Songs and Whispers headquarters. I will miss them too, especially Heiko and Arne. I feel like this company has been an answer to my prayers, in a lot of ways. They have helped me get re-inspired about playing music professionally.

Driving four and a half hours to Cologne was pretty straightforward. I listened to Marc Maron interview Neil Young on the WTF podcast. Good Stuff! I did not use a GPS navigation system until I arrived to the inner city of Cologne. I've been getting data overage messages again saying I'm $150 over my plan! *What the?* I've gotta call AT&T. Until then I'm using my data sparingly.

Did you know that Cologne is spelled K-ö-l-n in Germany? You won't find any road signs that say "Cologne," only signs that point to "Köln." I'll spell it Köln from now on as I think that's more fun. Besides, Cologne reminds me of the cologne that men wear which reminds me of business suits which reminds me that we live in a world of too many people trying to be someone they are not; trying to smell like something they are not.

I got to the venue called *"Heimathirsch"* on time. The entrance is like a bear cave down under the street! There was no one there at first, so I stood outside and waited until the owner named William arrived. William is a sturdy German man who speaks English pretty well, and is friendly and accommodating. I set up my gear. I ran my sound through their house PA.

"I'm not sure what to expect tonight. There's a football/soccer game on and the weather is so nice," William told me as I set up.

"I've heard that at almost every show on this tour. Shit happens," I consoled him. I never want to make club owners feel bad for taking a chance on having a concert at their venue. This business is unpredictable.

I was supposed to start playing at 8:15 p.m., but there were literally no customers in the bar at that time, just William, a very pretty and friendly bar tender named Anke (rhymes with Danke), and a friend of William's named Christian. William suggested I wait until more people came before I played, so we all sat down and had a beer.

As we sat and had a beer together I noticed Christian's shirt had a cow skull on it that said, "Las Cruces."

"Las Cruces," I said with excitement, "I love Las Cruces, New Mexico! Have you been?" I asked.

"No," he replied. "It's just a shirt I bought here in Köln."

Darn! I thought we'd have plenty to talk about, but nope.

We all exited the cave to the sidewalk above and stood outside with our beers and talked on this beautiful summer night in Köln. I thought about the park I had walked through a few hours previous after my sound check: all the children playing, and people living their lives out in the sunshine. Here we were, dwelling in this bar cave on this beautiful night like a bunch of depressed cases. Ha ha! The Rock-and-Roll Lifestyle...

As we stood on the sidewalk talking we could all see an outdoor cafe down the street full of people.

"You should just go over there and play to those people," William told me.

"Why? Isn't anyone over there playing music to them?" I asked William. "It'd be a perfect place for a busker."

"I'm not sure," William answered.

"What are the rules on busking here in Köln?" I asked William.

"You can do it for 30 minutes, then you have to move 500 meters away to another place," William said.

I was just about ready to get my instruments and play for the cafe when a man arrived to the bar. Anke went inside after him while we the rest of us stood on the sidewalk talking. Just as soon as the man entered the cave-bar, he exited. "He had come to hear you play," Anke told me, "but he will come back when he gets some food."

I went down into the cave-bar immediately and started playing. I was disappointed in myself. I should have played at 8:15 p.m. like all the promotion advertised. Dang! Starting a show on time is very important to me in my crusade to encourage people to come out and hear live music concerts by obscure artists! Here I was, breaking the number one rule to "Start On Time!" Ahhhh.

I played a long set for William, Christian, and Anke. I played all my songs in the mellowest way I could, careful not to disturb the chill atmosphere of the bar. (Nothing worse than walking into a bar to chill and being assaulted by loud, annoying music.) The man who had come to hear me never returned to the bar and never got to hear me play.

We all sat at the bar drinking beer after the show. People starting showing up at about 11:00 p.m. Apparently, there was a "DJ Shadow" concert happening tonight and a lot of people were there. The group that came in must have been a "group of regulars" I surmised by the way everyone greeted each other. I made the mistake of sitting too close to the bartender because people started handing me shots of Vodka. I don't drink Vodka because I got so hung over on it when I was about 14 years old that just the smell of it makes me want to puke, 25 years later! However, I sipped the first shot that was handed to me.

It's really tricky turning down a shot of Vodka that is handed to you by a stranger in Köln. They really mean well. It's almost as if they mean it as a gesture of accepting you into their clan. To turn it down would be to turn down their companionship. So, I slowly drank the first shot that came my way, but I am proud to report that I gave away any other shots that came my way. I didn't refuse them; I just let them sit at the bar until someone came along who looked like they wanted it.

As the night went on, I sat at the bar feeling more and more like a stranger. There was an old man who barely spoke English who sat down next to me. I think he was doing his best to be friendly, but whenever he'd ask my name, I'd reply "Fast Heart Mart," and he'd get so mad. I thought at one point he was going to start a fist fight with me, so I got up and sat somewhere else for a while until he asked me to come sit near him again.

I spoke to a younger guy at the bar. He spoke English well, though I could tell he was from Germany. First we talked about politics and "Donald Trump."

"It's all a soap opera," I told him. "The corporations are running the whole world now. The elections of politicians are just distractions from people taking action and fixing the world's problems themselves, one person at a time. Donald Trump is playing the antagonist in the TV Show of US politics that is produced and directed by world dominating corporations such as Monsanto. I like Bernie Sanders. I will vote for Bernie Sanders, but I know that if Barrack Obama can't do anything about the involvement of the USA military in the wars in the Middle East, how can anyone else. The only ones who can change the world are you and I," I concluded.

"Ok, let's talk about music," the man said. He seemed to find all my answers unsatisfactory. "What kind of music do you like?" has asked.

"I like good, innovative, honest, intimate, revealing, human music," I told him.

"Do you like Nirvana?" he asked.

"Of course!" I answered. I was excited because I thought we struck a common chord.

"I saw them here in Köln, in 1990, before anyone knew who they were. They opened for another band I went to see. I thought they were pretty good and then two months later they were *huge*."

"I have a similar story," I responded. I told him about my Math teacher being the same Math teacher Dave Grohl had. The man did not seem to want to hear my story. I couldn't help but think, "Well you didn't really take Nirvana seriously back in

1990, why would you take me seriously tonight. I'm a real musician, living out a real musician's life right before your eyes, but all you want to do is undermine me."

"Ok, let's talk about something else. Let's talk about what you're going to do next here in Germany," the man said.

"I'm going to play music in Frankfurt and meet up with a contact I've made and visit the Baha'i Temple in Frankfurt," I told him.

"What's the Baha'i Temple?" he asked. I told him about the Baha'i faith.

"OK, let's talk about something else," the man said. We had talked about politics, religion and rock n roll already! What else was there to talk about? "I can usually talk to anyone about anything," he assured me.

"Maybe I'm just a boring guy," I told him.

And with that we went our own ways.

Some where in the night, William came up and interjected himself in a conversation I was having with someone and said, "Fast Heart Mart has good music. Did you mean to be playing out of tune like that?" I didn't get a chance to respond. What did he mean by that? Ahhhhh, was I out of tune tonight? Am I the world's worst musician? Ugh.

I went outside to my car to grab some things so I could go to sleep. It was raining pretty heavily now. I saw the man who tried to talk to me about so many things out in the rain. His bike had fallen over while he was unlocking it. "Gute Nacht," I said as I scurried by trying not to get too wet in the rain. "Gute Nacht," he reluctantly responded.

I can be a great conversationalist, but I can also be a stick-in-the-mud. I guess tonight I was a stick in the mud for these Kölnians.

I was told many times by the Northern Germans, "Be careful of the Southern Germans. They are different. They're not really even German."

I'm not going to blame the people because I think they were very accommodating. William even bought four CDs and tipped me €50. I'm going to blame myself. I should have started the show on time and the night would have gone much better for me. It wasn't a bad night. I'm just disappointed with myself for not starting on time.

William let me sleep in the tiny apartment above the cave-bar. I climbed the spiral staircase and went to sleep.

The adventure continues…

(*Note to self: Always start the show on time! The show must go on, even if no one is there!*)

Days 33 - 37: Sightseein' & Chillin'

HERE I AM at the Baha'i House of Worship just outside of Frankfurt. I'm the tiny man at the bottom of the steps doing some much deserved chillin'.

I haven't written much lately because I took a break after the Songs and Whispers tour was over. I was staying with my new German family for a few days, relaxing and sightseeing. Thanks to them for letting me stay and taking care of me! Also, thanks to my New Mexican friend Julie England for connecting us!

As I visit the ruins of an old fortress in Germany from as far back as 800 AD, I'm reminded of how far humanity has come, yet how far we still have to go.

Day 74: Back Home, Safe & Sound

AFTER the Songs & Whispers tour ended, I played some shows in Finland, then flew back to the USA and visited family in Virginia. My cousin Sam's funeral happened the day after I arrived. His sister asked if I would say a eulogy. I had never written a eulogy before, but I felt like Sam was communicating with me as I wrote it early in the morning on the day of his funeral. I opened with a funny story of him when he was about ten. I talked about all the good things Sam brought to the world, such as loyalty, respect, music and humor. There will never be another Sam. We are all fortunate to have known him while he was here. I hope Sam meets me on the other side when it's time for me to die. After I said the eulogy for Sam, I played "I'll Fly Away" on the banjo. My friend Lance's father had also passed away. He was a sweet man who liked to hear me play the banjo. I played "Rocky Top" at his funeral as they carried the casket away. Perhaps it's my calling to visit with friends throughout the world and remind them to live passionately?

Day 75: Was It All Worth It?

YES. YES IT WAS! Very worth it!

This is my dream and I made it come true. I despise booking and promoting shows. For years I've prayed for someone to help me with booking and promotion. I just want to play music. For 30 days I was playing my music every night in different cities. I've done plenty of touring before, but this tour felt like the closest to being a bona fide "rock star." As far as I can tell, I think I broke even with my finances.

I've thought about it a lot, and I think my main reason for doing this tour was to re-inspire my "music career." I'm happy to report that I have definitely achieved this goal! I am now ready to play my music to the world as much as possible again.

I put "music career" in quotes because I'm still not sure if I can call what I've been doing with my music for the past 17 years, a "career." I think a "career" is usually defined as something that makes money. My "music career" has made some money, but overall, I have probably broken even after all the expenses of buying gear, traveling, promoting, etc. That's not a bad thing. At least I haven't racked up debt.

I can't say enough good things about the Songs and Whispers booking and promotion agency that booked the German tour for me! I was not sure about the whole concept at first, but now I am really into it.

Basically, Songs and Whispers booked and promoted about 30 shows in 30 days for me to play. In 30 days I had about three days off, but some days I had two shows a day. All I had to do was show up and play.

Here's how Songs and Whispers operates:
Note: This is the way that Songs and Whispers wants artists to understand their agency:
(http://songsandwhispers.blogspot.de/2012/08/terms-conditions.html)

This is the way I understand how Song sand Whispers works:

1. I paid Songs and Whispers a deposit of €400 for the booking and promotion of 30 shows in Germany. That's really cheap! Please let me know if you find a booking and promotion agency that will do anything close to this. The reason Songs and Whispers does this is because they put a lot of time, energy and materials into booking and promoting each artist on the tour. If an artist does not show up to do the tour, then the artist forfeits their €400 deposit to Songs and Whispers, therefore allowing the booking agency to recoup some of their costs.

2. I paid Songs and Whispers €600 to rent an apartment in Bremen, Germany for the month. That's also very reasonable for a month of lodging. Plus, the apartment is in a nice section of Bremen with a walking/biking/running trails nearby with trees and grass.

3. I played about 30 shows in 30 days. Songs and Whispers promotes the shows with flyers, radio spots and press, ahead of

time, so when I showed up to each town, people came out. Songs and Whispers seems to have quite a few fans that respect the brand in Germany now, which is nice because even if people haven't heard of me, they trust that Songs and Whispers is going to deliver a quality artist. Only about five of the shows had guaranteed money. Most of the money I made on the tour was from tips passing the hat towards the end of each performance. I also made a significant amount of money selling CDs.

4. At the end of the tour I added up all my tip money and gave Songs and Whispers 25%. This is where the €400 deposit comes in. I only had to pay Songs and Whispers 25% of my tip money if I made more than €1600. If I made less than €1600 they would owe me money from my €400 deposit.

Example:
- If I made €1500 in tips then Songs and Whispers would owe me €25 of my €400 deposit back.
- If I made €1600 then I would not owe them anything and they would not owe me anything.
- If I made €1700 then I would owe them €25 and so on.

Earnings:
Here is a list of my earnings from the Songs and Whispers tour. Keep in mind that my tour (June 2016) took place while the European Football Championship was going on, so a lot of people did not come out to the shows. Even with this lack of attendance I am still pleased with my results of my tour.

CD sales= € 645
Tips in the hat = €1,446
Guarantees = €500
Total Earnings = €2591
Expenses
Plane airfare: €1400

Car Rental: €1000 *(see note below about car rental)
Flat Rental: €600
Fuel for the Car: €450
CD costs: €170
Food: €0 ** (see note below about food)
Total Expenses: €3,620

* I think I got a good rate on my car rental? The guy I worked with was named Jan from Enterprise at the Hamburg airport. I drove 6,500 km (4,200 miles) while I was in Europe. When I turned in the car in Frankfurt the guy at the rental place asked me to confirm that this was true because he seemed a bit flabbergasted that I had driven this much in 30 days. However, I did not get charged extra. That is a lot of km/miles though. That's like driving from New York to Los Angeles, and back to New Mexico, and I only did Northern and Central Germany! Whoa!

** I don't count food as an "expense" because I'd have to eat whether I came on this tour or not. Also, since there is a flat/apartment with a grocery store close by, you don't have to eat out a lot if you don't want to. Furthermore, a lot of the venues provide food.

Ok, so as you can see, I lost about €1000 on this deal. However, I made it up by playing a few more shows in Finland after the Songs and Whispers tour. Friends who booked the additional shows also took care of my accommodations and travel. Thanks Finland friends!

Also, huge thanks to everyone who contributed to the fundraiser for this tour! I raised about $2,465 of the $3,600 goal.

I have no idea how I'll ever get the money together to do another trip like this, but it is my hope that I'll be able to do a European tour again next summer or sometime in the near future.

Ok. That's enough.

THE END

Printed in Great Britain
by Amazon